Dear Reader,

You hold in your hands the last book on which my father, Dr. D. James Kennedy, and his coauthor, Jerry Newcombe, collaborated before my dad passed away in September 2007.

The Presence of a Hidden God is a fitting finale to the nearly seventy books my father wrote or coauthored during his lifetime. He believed that Christianity is a reasonable faith and diligently studied the Scriptures as well as history, law, and science to equip him and others with evidence for the existence of God and the claims of Christianity.

That evidence—some of which he presents in this book—is compelling. In this, his last book, he shows how God makes Himself known to all of us, both in the world and in the person of His Son, Jesus Christ.

The Presence of a Hidden God answers objections to God put forward by doubters and skeptics. One thing about my father—he never shied away from honest objections. In fact, he loved to take on those kinds of questions.

I recall one evening when he visited in the home of a couple who were both well-educated professionals. He had the opportunity to respond to a long list of objections that they put to him. It grew very late. My father at one point took off his sport coat and rolled up his shirt sleeves to demonstrate his readiness to go the entire night if need be to satisfy their doubts. Finally, after their many questions had all been met with solid answers—like those given in this book—they bowed their heads to invite Christ to be their Lord and Savior.

I can say with confidence, both from my own experience in telling others about Jesus and from watching my father gently and convincingly answer objections, that Christianity is a reasonable faith. God makes Himself known, and He offers evidence for His existence.

I hope you will find comfort and fresh confidence in your own faith as you discover how God reveals Himself to man in this book. For my father, God is no longer hidden. For him, faith has now become glorious sight. But for us here below, he has left behind a powerful witness to help us see how God shows Himself in nature and in His Son.

Sincerely in Christ,

Jennifer Kennedy Cassidy
Member, Board of Directors
of Coral Ridge Ministries

Praise for
The Presence of a Hidden God

"This book demonstrates the rational coherence of the Christian faith. Atheism, which is supposedly based on reason, is shown to be inherently irrational. Only Christianity meets both the intellectual and intuitive longings of the human soul. Yes, the hidden God is present among us."

> —ERWIN W. LUTZER, PHD, senior pastor of the Moody Church,
> Chicago, IL, and author of *Christ Among Other Gods*
> and *Slandering Jesus*

"There are only two ways that we can know something: rational thought or revelation. When it comes to knowing God, history shows the first option is untrustworthy, as countless rational thinkers have asserted views of various gods that are either contradictory or irreconcilable. That leaves us with revelation, where God Himself chooses to reveal things hidden to our finite minds. This is the persuasive case made by D. James Kennedy and Jerry Newcombe in their excellent work *The Presence of a Hidden God*. With compelling narrative and excellent scholarship, they detail a revelation of God that is both awe inspiring and trustworthy. If you desire to make God known to those for whom He remains hidden, this is the book for you."

> —FRANK WRIGHT, PHD, president and CEO
> of National Religious Broadcasters

"*The Presence of a Hidden God* is a must-read and must-give-to-everyone book. It is the best book published in many years that presents the truth of God and Jesus Christ to unbelievers. The book takes off with insight and memorable stories that capture both mind and heart. I will quote *The Presence of a Hidden God* for years to come. I was moved to tears several times. I laughed out loud. This is the great evangelist Dr. D. James Kennedy's magnum opus due to the superb coauthoring of Jerry Newcombe. My suggestion is read it and be transformed!"

—TED BAEHR, chairman of the Christian Film & Television
Commission and publisher of *MovieGuide*®

"This, the final Kennedy-Newcombe book after twelve others, is probably their finest. It serves as a fitting capstone for Dr. Kennedy's extraordinary ministry, taking on the greatest theme that ever could be—God Himself—and with brilliant logic and shimmering illustrations proves not only His existence but how very threadbare are the arguments of today's resurgent atheists. But more, these pages also answer questions even the faithful may ask: Why does God seem hidden at times? Why does He permit evil? This book, defying the detractors and firming up the faithful, should be required reading to meet the challenges facing today's Christian."

—PAUL L. MAIER, professor of history, Western Michigan
University, and best-selling author

The
Presence of a
Hidden
GOD

Evidence for the God of the Bible

D. James Kennedy, PhD
and Jerry Newcombe

MULTNOMAH
BOOKS

THE PRESENCE OF A HIDDEN GOD
PUBLISHED BY MULTNOMAH BOOKS
12265 Oracle Boulevard, Suite 200
Colorado Springs, Colorado 80921
A division of Random House Inc.

ISBN: 978-1-60142-077-0

Library of Congress Cataloging-in-Publication Data
Kennedy, D. James (Dennis James), 1930-2007.
  The presence of a hidden God / D. James Kennedy, and Jerry Newcombe. — 1st ed.
    p. cm.
  Includes bibliographical references.
  ISBN 978-1-60142-077-0
  1. Presence of God. 2. Hidden God. 3. God (Christianity)—Knowableness.
I. Newcombe, Jerry. II. Title.
BT180.P6K46 2008
231—dc22
                                                    2007046466

Printed in the United States of America
2008—First Edition

10 9 8 7 6 5 4 3 2 1

SPECIAL SALES
Most WaterBrook Multnomah books are available in special quantity discounts when purchased in bulk by corporations, organizations, and special interest groups. Custom imprinting or excerpting can also be done to fit special needs. For information, please e-mail SpecialMarkets@WaterBrookMultnomah.com or call 1-800-603-7051.

Contents

Introduction

Truly You are God, who hide Yourself,
O God of Israel, the Savior!
ISAIAH 45:15

I s God hidden?

To hear skeptics speak, you would think so.

One of the most famous nonbelievers of the twentieth century was the British philosopher and mathematician Bertrand Russell. Well known for his skeptical stance, he even wrote a book titled *Why I Am Not a Christian*. Reportedly, when he was at death's door, he was asked about his readiness to die; what if it turned out there *was* a God after all?

In that case, Russell replied, he would ask the Almighty this question: "Why didn't You give us more evidence?"

His reaction prompted this comment from author and science teacher Ken Poppe:

> [Russell] seems to be positioning himself in case he needs to
> shift the blame of his disbelief to God for not being more con-
> vincing. (Hmmm. Did he never see a bright full moon setting
> in the cool, blue western sky, while the sun rose circular and

red through the eastern clouds? Did he never hold a new-born baby?)[1]

Who's correct: Russell or Poppe?

Indeed, is God hidden? Some people think so, but the problem lies with them, not with Him. "To the pure all things are pure, but to those who are defiled and unbelieving nothing is pure; but even their mind and conscience are defiled" (Titus 1:15). To the righteous, God is clearly there. To the unrighteous, God is absent—or worse, if He's there at all, He is cruel.

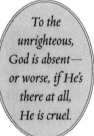

To the unrighteous, God is absent— or worse, if He's there at all, He is cruel.

God is not really hidden; He just appears so to those who don't know Him. Yet even believers sometimes feel that He hides His face and seems absent when we need Him most.

Blaise Pascal put it this way: "What can be seen on earth indicates neither the total absence of God nor his manifest presence, but rather the presence of a hidden God."[2] Likewise the classic hymn "Holy, Holy, Holy" reminds us that the darkness may seem to hide God:

> Holy, holy, holy! though the darkness hide Thee,
> Though the eye of sinful man Thy glory may not see;
> Only Thou art holy; there is none beside Thee;
> Perfect in power, in love, and purity.[3]

The "eye of sinful man" is unable to perceive the Lord or His glory. In other words, to a blind man God may seem hidden, but to those whose eyes He has opened, He isn't hidden at all. He has clearly revealed Himself in Jesus Christ.

In every language, every tribe, and every culture, we find a word for God. He has not left Himself without a witness, nor is there any-where on earth where His fingerprints are absent.

Pascal reflected on God's manner of revealing Himself to us through Christ:

> Since so many have become unworthy of his mercy, he wished to deprive them of the good that they did not desire. It was therefore not right that [Christ] should appear before them in a manner that was obviously divine and absolutely bound to convince all mankind. Neither was it right that his coming should be in such hiddenness that he could not be recognized even by those who sincerely looked for him. But he wished to make himself perfectly recognizable to such.[4]

This is reminiscent of a promise from Jesus: "If anyone chooses to do God's will, he will find out whether my teaching comes from God" (John 7:17, NIV).

MILITANT ATHEISM

God has more than His share of critics. If He could be sued, there are plenty of people who would bring Him before the bar.

Today there has arisen a virulent form of atheism. Militant atheists are on the march. One of them, Sam Harris, wrote a book entitled *Letter to a Christian Nation,* essentially appealing to us to become like the failed Soviet Union. (He doesn't actually word it that way, but that's the effect of his message.) His book and a handful of other virulent anti-Christian creeds have made it onto the *New York Times* bestseller list.

One of the great ironies of militant atheists is how their whole lives seem to be consumed in fighting what they claim doesn't exist.

I think if they truly did *not* believe God existed, they wouldn't really care about the topic and would simply look down their noses at us poor slobs who do believe in Him. However, these militant atheists are consumed with a passion to erase all traces of God.

A lot of these atheist books blur the distinction between Christianity and Islam. They cite the horrible atrocities done in the name of religion (mostly by Islamic extremists) and argue that the problem is with religion in general. Meanwhile, they ignore the horrible atrocities committed by atheists, who have the bloodiest track record in history, bar none.

I suspect they do know, deep down, there's a God.

Some of these modern atheists are so emotionally charged on the issue that it makes me suspect they indeed do know, deep down, there's a God. Again, if they *really* didn't believe in Him, they wouldn't care so much. We can see the animus against God in lawsuit after lawsuit contesting any public acknowledgment of God (such as the Ten Commandments on a courtroom wall).

There *is* a God. He made us. He has certain standards of right and wrong that He has revealed. We are accountable to Him.

If a blind man denies reality just because he can't see it, does that mean it isn't there?

Meanwhile, where *is* God? Even believers sometimes wonder that during times of pain.

THE HIDDENNESS OF GOD
IN THE LIFE OF THE BELIEVER

C. S. Lewis, the greatest Christian writer of the twentieth century, once made this observation: "The 'hiddenness' of God perhaps presses most painfully on those who are in another way nearest to

Him, and therefore God Himself, made man, will of all men be by God most forsaken?"[5]

So it was that Jesus Himself, on the cross, cried out, "My God, My God, why have You forsaken Me?" (Mark 15:34). If God's Son made David's words His own and cried out to His Father in the anguish and loneliness of His soul, how much more should we do so in our times of anguish? It's not wrong to feel forsaken. Throughout the Scriptures we see God's saints crying out to Him when He seems totally absent. Consider God's children in Egypt and in the wilderness, or Hannah when she couldn't conceive a child, or David when he hid from Saul in a cave, or Jonah in the belly of the fish. All cried out to God.

When we come to God in our joy, praising and thanking Him, we find open arms. But in our times of greatest need, sometimes heaven seems shut tight. We plead and cry, and even if God did answer, we probably couldn't hear it. When all earthly help is gone and we knock on God's door, there seems to be only silence. The God of love, who had been so real to us during times of plenty, seems out of reach now. So we hammer on His door. We kick and yell, until we eventually give up.

Then, when we're finally quiet, we see dawn coming. God has put the answer into nature itself. Morning always follows night. Spring always comes, no matter how dark and cold and long the winter seems. There are such seasons in the spiritual lives of believers too.

Sometimes our tree is bare and seems dead.

Sometimes we're used by God and the fruit is plentiful. Other times our tree is bare and seems dead. There are times of growth and times of flowering. If we let the Master Gardener dig around and fertilize, our tree will bear fruit again. So often God is behind the scenes, working out His good purpose for us.

GOD REVEALED IN CHRIST

First and foremost, God is found in Jesus Christ, as the Savior Himself proclaimed: "No one knows…the Father except the Son, and the one to whom the Son wills to reveal Him" (Matthew 11:27). The goal of this book is to expound on that truth and others related to it.

As British author George MacDonald once put it, "God hides nothing. His very work from the beginning is *revelation*—a casting aside of veil after veil, a showing unto men of truth after truth. On and on from fact divine he advances, until at length in his son Jesus he unveils his very face."[6]

If with all our hearts we seek the Lord, we *will* find Him. Join me on a journey of discovery, wherein we'll see that the so-called hidden God is not hidden after all.

In the first part of this book, we'll take a look at how God has revealed Himself in His creation. Next, in part 2, we'll look at how He has revealed Himself through His Son. Part 3 will explore ways we can experience the God who isn't hidden after all. Finally, in part 4, we'll look at shadows that obscure God and may seem to hide His face from us.

Let the journey begin.

PART I

IS GOD
HIDDEN?

Evidence for God

The heavens declare the glory of God;
And the firmament shows His handiwork.
PSALM 19:1

Two little droplets of water are next to each other at the Continental Divide. One trickles east, the other west. In a moment they're an inch apart, then a foot apart. It isn't long before they're a mile apart. Eventually they're a continent apart—thousands of miles.

So it is with the difference between belief in God and unbelief.

More key beliefs flow from the following question than from any other issue: is there a God or not? Why is that question so pivotal? Because belief in God, or disbelief in Him, is the starting point of all faith systems. Even atheism is a faith system. Atheism is based on certain assumptions; so also is theism. Neither assumption can be proved, but as we'll see later, there's far more evidence *for* God than against Him.

If you believe the world essentially created itself, that's a far different starting point than believing in a self-sufficient Supreme Being who always was, is, and ever will be. In essence, the question is, is God self-sufficient and always existing, or is the universe self-sufficient and always existing? Where you start from virtually always determines where you'll end up.

The Bible says, "The fool has said in his heart, 'There is no God'" (Psalms 14:1; 53:1). Every culture, every tribe, and every nation has

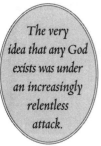

The very idea that any God exists was under an increasingly relentless attack.

an idea about God. Everyone knows God exists. But some people foolishly suppress that fact.

Through most of the last century, the very idea that any God exists was under an increasingly relentless attack, so much so that the twentieth century has been called the century of atheism. That trend has continued into this century and the new

millennium. So let's look at the evidence for God's existence.

THE CORE QUESTION

Is there a God, or is there not? In its importance, that question eclipses all others that humanity might ask.

The late Dr. Mortimer J. Adler was a philosopher and the editor in chief of *The Great Books of the Western World,* sixty volumes of the greatest writings of the greatest minds in Western history. These volumes go all the way back to the best of the ancient Greek writers and continue through writers of modern times. Dr. Adler wrote that "with the exception of certain mathematicians and physicists," almost all the authors in the *Great Books* deal in some way with the subject of God. "The reason," he said, "is obvious":

> More consequences for thought and action follow the affirma-
> tion or denial of God than the answering of any other basic
> question. The whole tenor of human life is affected by
> whether men regard themselves as the supreme being in the

universe, or acknowledge a superhuman being whom they conceive of as an object of fear or love and a force to be defied, or a Lord to be obeyed.[1]

Whether a person believes in God will make more difference than anything else in his thoughts, his life, and his eternal destiny.

A number of years ago I was a guest on television's *The Merv Griffin Show*. We were talking about prayer in schools, and Griffin said, "What good is a couple of minutes of prayer going to do, anyway? What difference does it make?" It makes a great deal of difference, if one believes in God. When one prays or a class of students prays, they're affirming that a higher authority than the state controls the schools. The state doesn't like that, and secular man doesn't like that, but the students are acknowledging there's a God.

Does it really make any difference?

OUT OF THE MOUTHS OF BABES

The entire tenor of our lives will be completely affected by the answer we give to this profound question: is there a God? It has been asked for countless centuries, not only by scholars and educators, but even by children, who have some interesting ways of asking it. Take this letter, for example:

Dear God,

Are you real? Some people don't believe it. If you are you better do something quick.

Harriet Ann[2]

Or this from a young but cautious skeptic:

> Dear Mr. God,
>
> How do you feel about people who don't believe in you? Somebody else wants to know.
>
>> A friend,
>> Neil[3]

Or this from Charlene:

> Dear God,
>
> How did you know you were God?[4]

Only a child would think of that.

TWO REVOLUTIONS

So much depends on whether we believe in God. As I have said, there was a massive effort in the twentieth century to do away with belief in God. But the times they are achangin'. The tide is turning. There's a shift in the wind.

The pillars of secularism, atheism, and materialism are crumbling from a two-pronged attack. First, they're crumbling from the advance of the gospel as it is proclaimed by tens of millions of Christians all over the world, and people are being converted to Christ in astronomically increasing numbers. Second, at the highest intellectual levels, increasing numbers of minds are realizing that all this secularism, all this atheism, and all this materialism have been dead wrong.

One scientist, Dr. James Reid, in his book *God, the Atom, and the Universe,* puts it this way:

> Science is preparing a surprise for mankind. At least it will be a surprise for those who have doubts about the Bible and its God. It will also come as a surprise for those who are laboring under the misapprehension that science has undermined the Bible. In fact, it may even shock some scientists, who may be startled to find that their newly uncovered facts, or accepted theory, provide still another link in the chain of evidence that is showing that the facts of the universe support the Bible's statements—including creation.[5]

He goes on to say that for years he endeavored unsuccessfully to find support for the Bible in science under the Newtonian concepts of physics. However, he noted how Newtonian concepts have given way to the whole idea of quantum physics—quantum theory, quantum mechanics—which has totally transformed the scientific world. Now he's discovering that true science supports the statements of the Scripture. That's encouraging.

The evidence for this is ironic. The two great revolutions that tended to turn mankind away from God have been, first, the Copernican revolution in astronomy, which began five hundred years ago, and, second, the Darwinian revolution in biology, which began in the eighteen hundreds.

Copernicus discovered that the Earth was not the center of the universe. The Bible doesn't teach that the Earth is the center of the universe, but Ptolemy had taught that the Earth was the center of the solar system and that all the planets, the sun, and the stars revolved around it. This had been accepted as fact by the Catholic Church (to their great embarrassment later).

Copernicus came to realize this wasn't the case. In fact, he revealed that the Earth moved around the sun, as did the rest of the planets, and that the stars didn't revolve around the Earth either. Eventually humanity came to realize the Earth is a rather small planet on the fringes of a rather insignificant galaxy known as the Milky Way. Therefore the idea that people held a significant position in the universe began to slide downhill.

The idea that people held a significant position in the universe began to slide downhill.

It was indeed a steep slide. People like the late Stephen Jay Gould of Harvard, an evolutionist and atheist, have pointed out that humanity has no more significance than an "accidental twig."[6] In other words, we're of no significance at all. This is the final fruit of the Copernican revolution as far as unbelievers are concerned.

But recall again what the Bible tells us: "The fool has said in his heart, 'There is no God' " (Psalms 14:1; 53:1). And this: "He who sits in the heavens shall laugh" (2:4).

I find a rather delicious irony here. In 1973 the five hundredth anniversary of the birth of Copernicus was celebrated. At that time unbelieving scientists celebrated the Copernican revolution, and what they were celebrating was the demise of mankind and, more importantly, the demise of God. Although Copernicus himself was a Christian believer, his cause has been embraced by unbelievers who mistakenly think the Polish astronomer decimated the biblical understanding of the universe. (As I say, he did prove false the Ptolemaic view but not the scriptural view.)

At that 1973 celebration in Krakow, Poland, where Copernicus was born, one of those present was a highly reputed astrophysicist from the University of Oxford, Professor Brandon Carter. He had been invited to read a scientific paper on that occasion. In it, he noted his recent discovery of certain strange and almost inexplicable things in the world of particle physics and astronomy that he didn't quite know what to do with. Why? Because they all seemed to indicate that our world—indeed the whole universe—had been constructed and maintained for a *purpose*. That purpose was the bringing out, in due time, of intelligent life on this planet—namely, mankind.

To evolutionists, *purpose* is among the dirtiest of words. In their minds everything is merely an accident, the accidental concatenation of certain amino acids in an ancient and primordial slime that led to human beings. There's no purpose or teleology—an end to anything. In contrast, as Christians we believe God created the world and humanity for a purpose. This idea is anathema to the unbeliever.

But Professor Carter noted such things as consistent symmetry in the mathematical equation for gravity and the fact that if the mass of the proton were just a fraction larger or smaller, the entire solar system would collapse. All these things, he said, point to the fact that somehow this universe appears to have been designed for mankind. He called this the Anthropic Principle. *Anthropos* is the Greek word for "man." The Anthropic Principle, therefore, is the "man" principle. So at the five hundredth anniversary of the Copernican revolution, when the final spike was being driven into the significance of man, the Anthropic Principle was born.

The discoveries noted by Professor Carter have been followed by scores of discoveries from other scientists, like a snowball turning into an avalanche. Today virtually no scientist can deny the Anthropic Principle—the fact that this world was made with a purpose and that purpose was mankind. For example, two brilliant scientists, Guillermo Gonzalez and Jay Richards, who embrace intelligent design, have written a book, *The Privileged Planet*, documenting how Earth has been uniquely positioned to sustain human life.[7]

Though human beings may not geographically be in the center of the universe, we're in the center of God's heart, and He made all of the universe for us.

Truly it is the fool who has said there is no God.

You probably learned in school about the nebular hypothesis concerning the formation of the solar system. The hypothesis was set forth by Pierre Simon Laplace, a notable scientist and astronomer who wrote a five-volume work on "celestial mechanics" and whose knowledge of the mechanics of the universe was absolutely encyclopedic. I wonder how many of us ever heard the following quote from Laplace. (I never did.) Listen to this: "The proof in favor of an intelligent God as the author of creation stands as infinity to unity against any other hypothesis of ultimate causation."[8]

The odds that God created the world are infinitely high.

In other words, the odds that God created the world are infinitely high, compared to essentially zero. It isn't possible to give a greater contrast than infinity to unity—from an infinite number to zero. Pierre Simon Laplace said it is infinitely more probable that a set of writing implements thrown promiscuously against a huge parchment would produce Homer's *Iliad* than that the creation originated by any cause other than God.[9]

Sir James Jeans, one of the greatest astronomers of modern times, said that the more he studied the universe, the more the universe seemed to him to be one gigantic thought of a great mathematician. It has meaning, symmetry, and reason.[10]

Many other factors have also shown the teleology, or purpose, of the world in which we live. Some of them are more commonplace than the ones now being discovered in these esoteric realms of particle physics and astronomy. But just consider some rather close, down-to-earth concepts—like the moon. We all look at the moon, admire the moon, sing about the moon. The moon in June brings out tunes and all that, but what does the moon really mean to us?

If there were no moon, there would be no you. For the moon is God's maid for Earth. It cleans up the oceans with its tides. Without those tides and without the moon, all our shores and all our bays would be filled with billions of tons of garbage and debris. The highest-priced real estate would be as far from a seashore as you could get, especially the leeward shore.

Furthermore, the moon mixes the atmosphere. Just as it works on the sea, it works on the atmosphere and mixes oxygen into the water as the waves break on the shore. Upon that aerated water depends the life of the sea's plankton, which provides the basis of the ground level of the whole food chain, without which we all would die. The moon, which just "accidentally" happens to be there, also just "accidentally" happens to be the right size and the right distance from the Earth for these things to happen as they do.

Consider our atmosphere further. It's made of 78 percent nitrogen, 21 percent oxygen, and 1 percent of a few other things. Think about the nitrogen for a moment. Most of our atmosphere is nitrogen. Nitrogen, when mixed with almost anything, becomes poisonous to us. Happily, atmospheric nitrogen is extraordinarily inert. It doesn't mix with much of anything. That's good...or is it? Without nitrogen there would be no plants. So how did God get the nitrogen to mix into the soil for the plants to feed on without mixing it into the air we breathe, which would kill us? By having a hundred thousand strokes of lightning every day around the globe. The lightning alters molecular atmospheric nitrogen into compounds like ammonia and nitrates, which are carried to the ground by rain. That system produces a hundred million tons of nitrogen plant food every year and keeps this world going. So the next time you're startled by a bolt of lightning, stop and think: were it not for that, you wouldn't be alive for long.

How little we think about what God has done and continues to do every day for our lives.

Consider the matter of dust, the greatest bane to a person with allergies. It causes sneezing and runny eyes and many other uncomfortable things. It's a pain in the neck to people who like to keep their homes or offices clean. The next time you dust a table or desk or bookshelf, I hope you'll thank God for it. If it weren't for dust, you wouldn't be alive. Why is that?

Let's look at two things dust does. One is merely cosmetic. If you go twenty-five miles straight up into the atmosphere, there's no dust. But there's also no blue sky. It's pitch black. It's the effect of dust on light in our atmosphere that makes the sky blue. We wouldn't be able to sing songs about the blue skies were it not for dust. Have you ever noticed pictures taken on the moon? It has black skies.

But dust does something more important: every drop of rain contains eight million tiny droplets of water, and each of those eight million droplets of water is wrapped around a tiny speck of dust. If it weren't for dust, it would never rain. If it never rained, this whole world would turn into a Sahara desert, and all of us would die. So thank God the next time you dust your table or even sneeze.

I could go on and on. It's almost endless the way God has provided this nest for His creatures and maintains it and cares for it century after century, because He's the God who works all things for our good. How marvelous, indeed, He is.

Conclusion

The story is told of Athanasius Kircher, a devout Christian astronomer, and an atheist acquaintance with whom he often argued. Kircher decided to construct a complex working model of the solar system showing the sun with the planets circling around it. It was a wonder to behold. One day his atheist friend came into his study and was amazed and intrigued by the model's incredible complexity. He exclaimed, "How beautiful it is. Who made it?"

Kircher replied, "No one made it; it made itself."

The atheist looked at him and said, "That's absurd. You don't expect me to believe that, do you?"

Kircher said, "No, I don't. But what's even more absurd is that's what you believe about the real solar system, which is vastly more complex than this simple model."[11]

When we consider the complexity of God's handiwork in the universe, we begin to see that He's not quite so hidden as the skeptics assert. For as David wrote, "The heavens declare the glory of God; and the firmament shows His handiwork" (Psalm 19:1).

More Evidence for God

I would seek God,
and to God I would commit my cause—who does great things,
and unsearchable, marvelous things without number.

JOB 5:8–9

At the beginning of his *Confessions* addressed to God, Saint Augustine wrote this: "You made us for yourself, and our hearts find no peace until they rest in you."[1] This maxim that the human heart is a God-shaped blank that only God can fill has been around for almost seventeen hundred years, but I'm afraid there aren't too many people familiar with it today. Millions are trying to fill their hearts with everything except God, and they don't succeed. Consequently we've seen suicide become endemic, euthanasia on the march, and mental disorders of all kinds, depression, despair, and hopelessness everywhere.

What an incredible truth: only God can fill that void. You cannot run a jet plane with tomato juice, and you cannot fill the God-shaped void of the human heart—created by Him and for Him—with anything else but Him.

> *What are you trying to fill the deep desires of your heart with?*

What are you trying to fill the deep desires of your heart with? Where are you seeking your satisfaction, your happiness? Is it in God, or is it in some of the baubles of this earth? Money? Fame? Fortune? Fun? Relaxation? These are just a few of the substitutes people without God have used to try to fill their hearts. Strangely, though we live in a time when the very pillars of atheism are crumbling, there are still people who say there is no God to fill that vacuum in the human heart. Yet this is becoming a more and more difficult challenge for them.

Dr. Robert Jastrow is a name you ought to be familiar with. Virtually every scientist in the world knows who he is. He's the founder and former director of the Goddard Institute for Space Studies at NASA and one of the world's great astronomers. In his blockbuster book *God and the Astronomers,* he writes, "Strange developments are going on in astronomy. They are fascinating partly because of their theological implications, and partly because of the peculiar reactions of scientists."[2]

One of the more recent developments Jastrow refers to was the discovery that the universe had a beginning. After the acceptance of Darwinism, most scientists had asserted that the universe was eternal, because if there was a beginning, there had to be a Beginner. And most scientists were not ready to accept that.

The idea that the world had a beginning went down hard for some. Early in the twentieth century, the great English astronomer Sir Arthur Stanley Eddington declared, "The notion of a beginning is repugnant."[3] Such repugnance, of course, is not an intellectual concept but an emotional reaction. Why should an astronomer react emotionally to a scientific discovery unless his heart is involved? Even Albert Einstein wrote, "Such possibilities seem senseless."[4] Until he saw it with his own eyes, he wouldn't believe it, though eventually he did come to believe that the world had a beginning.

Jastrow also wrote this: "The scientist has scaled the mountains of ignorance; he is about to conquer the highest peak; as he pulls himself over the final rock, he is greeted by a band of theologians who have been sitting there for centuries."[5]

Many others like Jastrow are expressing similar thoughts, some of which are included in a monumental book from sixty notable scientists, including twenty-four Nobel prize winners. The title is *Cosmos, Bios, Theos* from the Greek words for "universe," "life," and "God." The coeditor of the book, Yale physicist Henry Margenau, concludes there is "only one convincing answer" for the intricate laws existing in nature. And that one convincing answer is "creation by an omnipotent-omniscient God."[6]

More and more pillars of atheism are crumbling. That doesn't mean atheists are necessarily any less atheistic; it just means, as Norman Geisler says, there's less reason for there to be any atheists at all.[7] But there will always be some who are willing to stand up and debate God's existence.

AN ATHEIST'S ARGUMENT

I received a copy of the audiotapes of a debate between a noted theologian and a noted atheist. The atheist, a university professor and president of a number of various atheistic associations, gave fascinating arguments. He claimed that an atheist is not one who denies God's existence or disbelieves in God but merely someone who has examined the theistic arguments in favor of God and found them wanting. Why would he make such an assertion?

I went to one dictionary after another to see how *atheist* is defined. Repeatedly it's defined simply as one who disbelieves or denies the existence of God. Each source said exactly the same thing, the very thing the atheist debater denied. Why would he do that?

I believe it's because at least some atheists have learned their lesson.

Quite a few years ago I was invited to debate an atheist during three hours of radio time. The first thing I asked this doctor was, "Are you an atheist?"

He said, "Yes."

I said, "Do you deny the existence of God?"

He said, "Oh, absolutely."

I said, "Wonderful. I suppose you understand that atheism is irrational."

He said, "What do you mean? Of course not."

I said, "Atheism, of course, is a universal negative. *Atheism* comes from the two words *theos,* which means 'God,' and the Greek negative particle *a-,* which makes it 'no God.' Atheism says there is no God."

Everyone who has studied logic knows what my friend on the radio didn't know: it's impossible to prove a universal negative. If you say there's no such thing in the entire universe as little green men, let me assure you, you can't possibly prove it. Should you travel to every planet and every star, and inside every star, and through every galaxy in the entire universe and come back and tell me you didn't see one, I would simply say to you, "Well, you missed him. While you were going that way, he was zigging this way."

Atheism is a logical contradiction.

You would have to examine every single part of the universe *at the same time.* I'll say it again: it's impossible, according to the laws of logic, to prove any universal negative. A universal negative is when you say, "There's no such thing in the universe as..."—as little green men, or angels, or God. Therefore, atheism is a logical contradiction, and to affirm a logical contradiction is irrational.

I said, "Dear sir, you are an irrational man."

All atheists pride themselves on being quite rational. Our friend tried to redefine the term right off, because he knew he had no chance of proving real atheism to be true.

He started with one of the classic proofs of the existence of God called the cosmological argument (*cosmos* means "the universe")—the argument from the causation of the entire universe. He first quoted the familiar cosmological argument by which Christians often assert that God exists: "Everything must have a cause. The universe is something. Therefore, it must have a cause, and that cause must be God." He countered, "If that's the case, then God, being 'something,' must also have a cause. So who caused God?"

He was evading the point, because if something caused God, the immediate next question would be "Who caused the something that caused God?" And then "Who caused *that* something that caused the something that caused God?" It leads you to an infinite regress, which isn't possible, especially since we know the universe is not eternal.

But the man misquoted the initial statement. The argument is not "Everything must have a cause" but "Every *effect* must have a cause sufficient to account for that effect." God is not an effect, and God did not need a cause. God is an eternal being who has never *not* existed.

A woman once said to seminary professor Dr. Manford Gutzke, "My six-year-old daughter wants to know who created God."

He replied, "Just tell her nobody created God; He has always existed and will always exist."

"But she's only six years old. She won't understand that."

"That's all right," Dr. Gutzke said. "When she gets to be sixty years old, she still won't understand it, but you tell her anyway, because it's the truth."

If we could wrap our minds around the infinite God, we would be greater than He is. We can apprehend Him, but we cannot comprehend Him entirely. So God has always existed and needs no cause at all.

TELEOLOGICAL ARGUMENT

The atheist on the radio program with me then tried to get rid of what is called the teleological argument. The Greek word *telos* means "end." *Teleological* has to do with examining something for ends, for purpose, or for design. (We touched briefly on this in the last chapter.) Whenever we see anything that appears to have been designed to accomplish a certain purpose, we inevitably believe there's intelligence behind it. If you look at an incredibly complicated machine, you instinctively know someone designed it to perform the functions it is obviously performing.

The atheist tried to dismiss this in cavalier fashion by simply twisting words around. But the teleological argument is absolutely abundant. We see proof of God's design everywhere—every day and night in the sky, for example. Again to quote David in Psalm 19, "The heavens declare the glory of God.... Day unto day utters speech, and night unto night reveals knowledge" (verses 1–2).

We also see in the human body incredible evidence of design for an end. Take the human eye. It contains four hundred million cones, three hundred million minute fibers, and fifty million tiny nerves called "rods"—some to show us black and white, others to show us color. Interestingly, every one of those millions of cones, fibers, and rods adjust themselves automatically. All you have to do is look at a rose, and all seven hundred fifty million of them go to work—without one thought on your part—to make sure you see the color and the shade and the shape of that rose. Isn't "chance" wonderful? That's what the atheist *must* say. But the truth is, isn't God wonderful?

By the way, the atheist on the radio also derided Christians for starting with the Bible—as the Word of God—to prove God's existence. He was simply setting up another straw man. But the fact is, if you read the Bible carefully, you discover there are more than two thousand specific predictive prophecies that have already been fulfilled—an absolutely miraculous occurrence that has no parallel in any other writing on the face of this earth. Therefore, one must conclude there's some supernatural agency behind it, since no mere human writing has ever been able to do anything within a thousandth of that. Therefore, we come to understand that the Bible is, indeed, the Word of God.

The truth is, isn't God wonderful?

PASCAL'S WAGER

Blaise Pascal, who lived in the early seventeenth century in France, was a great Christian and a brilliant theologian, mathematician, and scholar. One of his reflections has come to be called Pascal's wager.

To the extent that faith in God—or lack of it—is a "bet" about God's existence, Pascal demonstrated that it was safer and superior to risk one's life on God's existence than to bet against it. For if there is no God or eternal life and we simply cease to exist when we die, then we've lost nothing by having either believed or not believed in God during our time on earth. But if there *is* a God so that at death believers go to heaven and unbelievers go to hell, then there's absolutely everything to lose from wagering that He doesn't exist. Pascal concluded that no intelligent person should fail to see this.

However, my atheist friend took that and twisted it around. He said Pascal's wager meant that we ought to bet there is *a* god—a flawed and weak conclusion, he said, because you still have to choose which religion and which god. Maybe the god you get is an irrational god who sends good people to hell and bad people to heaven.

Of course, the atheist's reasoning was totally fallacious. Pascal was a Christian living in the midst of a Christian milieu, and he talked about not *a* god, but *the* God, the Christian God, the God of the Bible, who is neither irrational nor capricious in His acts.

WANTING IT NOT TO BE TRUE

Over and over again we see that the unbeliever's arguments will not hold water.

Although there have been many credible explanations to demonstrate the logic of God's existence, philosophers like David Hume, John Stuart Mill, and Bertrand Russell have tried to disprove them. Their findings aren't convincing to me or to millions of other Christians or to many scholars who have examined them. But I'm afraid some people simply don't want such explanations to be true, don't want to believe God exists—simply because of their own sin.

Aldous Huxley, the famous twentieth-century humanist, once observed that disbelief in God allowed for sexual liberation. By rejecting God, unbelievers could therefore embrace "the philosophy of meaninglessness" and be freed from the old moral restraints. Here's what Huxley wrote in *Ends and Means* in 1937:

> For myself as, no doubt, for most of my contemporaries, the philosophy of meaninglessness was essentially an instrument of liberation. The liberation we desired was simultaneously liberation from a certain political and economic system and liberation from a certain system of morality. We objected to the morality because it interfered with our sexual freedom;

we objected to the political and economic system because it was unjust. The supporters of these systems claimed that in some way they embodied the meaning (a Christian meaning, they insisted) of the world. There was one admirably simple method of confuting these people and at the same time justifying ourselves in our political and erotic revolt: we could deny that the world had any meaning whatsoever.[8]

Huxley's statements here are summed up by Christian apologist Ravi Zacharias in these words: "I want this world not to have meaning because it frees me to my own passions and to my own sensually driven life."[9]

There's an irony here lost on many to this day. God's rules for sex are for *our good*. God is the creator of sex. He's the one who fashioned all those nerve endings. In designing the way the human race is propagated, God could easily have made our procreation nothing more than an act of drudgery. Instead, the Lord designed us for finding pleasure in sexual intimacy and the conception of human life. And God's rules regarding sex are not oppressive but quite simple: it's to be confined to a man and a woman in marriage. And though most of the world doesn't realize this, studies have shown that, in general, committed Christian married couples enjoy the best sex.[10]

> *The atheist thinks God is trying to hold back from us something good.*

But the atheist rejects God, thinking that God is trying to hold back from us something good (sexual pleasure in particular). Little does the atheist know that his beliefs defeat his own purpose. God made sex, and His rules lead to the best and most satisfying sex.

Those who reject God often have a vested interest in doing so, and their sexual sin is the main reason. Take the example of Bertrand

Russell, one of the twentieth century's greatest philosophers. He was also a flagrant adulterer. He said his atheism freed him up not to his intellectual studies but to his erotic desires. On one occasion when a good friend invited him to his beautiful mansion for the weekend, Russell seduced his friend's sixteen-year-old daughter.[11]

It is just as Paul explains about such people: "And even as they did not like to retain God in their knowledge, God gave them over to a debased mind, to do those things which are not fitting" (Romans 1:28).

AN EMOTIONAL RESPONSE

Have you ever noticed how emotional some people get in their rejection of God? Granted, as children some had such an awful experience at the hands of a church authority that as adults they want nothing to do with the Lord in any way. Tragically, such stories seem to be legion. Ministers, elders, deacons, priests, and nuns who have forever turned off a child to faith in the Lord will pay an awful price. For Jesus said, "Whoever causes one of these little ones who believe in Me to sin, it would be better for him if a millstone were hung around his neck, and he were drowned in the depth of the sea" (Matthew 18:6).

I heard about a Unitarian who confided to an evangelical friend that many of his co-religionists should seek therapy for harmful childhood experiences involving the mainstream church. For example, a nun at a Catholic school whacked children on their hands repeatedly in front of the whole class, and they were humiliated. They hate the church, and now they seek alternative forms of spirituality. Many people had terrible experiences in the church when they were young. For example, a child grows up with overly strict and judgmental church-going parents, or an altar boy is seduced by an errant priest. Understandably, these victims of abuse now hate the church and seek alternative forms of spirituality. Furthermore, they reject God as He has revealed Himself in Scripture.

Meanwhile, there are many who fight against God, against the Word of God, and against any public expression of religion or public acknowledgment of God with all the energy they have. Why? I believe it's because of the conviction of sin. They hate those Ten Commandments plaques on the courtroom walls because they themselves are in sin, committing adultery or stealing or whatever.

Why do atheist groups fight with all their being against something they supposedly think doesn't exist? I mentioned earlier that if they really believed God doesn't exist, they would dismiss the idea and simply feel sorry for those miserable suckers who do believe. Why are they consumed in fighting something if they're truly convinced it isn't there?

I believe they *know* God is there but dread the consequences. This is why David observes, "The fool has said in his heart, 'There is no God.' They are corrupt, they have done abominable works, there is none who does good" (Psalm 14:1). This is why God is hidden to some and will remain hidden all the days of their lives if they don't repent and turn to Jesus.

Apologetics can only go so far. If someone rejects the truth of God and suppresses it in his heart, his foolish heart gets darkened. Romans 1 so clearly traces this. The unbeliever rejects the knowledge of God and is not thankful to God. As his heart becomes darker, he turns to worshiping things that are not God, creeping things that God has made. The person also turns to perverted sexuality, including homosexuality and lesbianism. As people degenerate further, they do everything in their power to get society's acceptance for their sin.

Reading Romans 1:18–32 is like reading a summary of today's culture war and the emotional reactions it evokes. Disbelief in God is often an emotional thing that has nothing to do with the facts. To paraphrase Jesus, light has come into the world, but people prefer darkness because their deeds are evil (see John 3:19).

DOING AWAY WITH EVIL

One of the most frequent arguments against God's existence is the prevalence of evil we see all around us in this world. If God exists and is truly good, He would surely want to do away with evil, and if He's truly omnipotent, He *would* in fact do away with it. But since evil clearly exists, they therefore conclude there is no God—or at least not one who's both good and all-powerful.

Is their conclusion answerable?

Yes. It's simple. When they complain that God hasn't done away with evil, there's one important word missing—the word *yet*. God has not *yet* done away with evil, but He has clearly revealed to us in His Word that He *will* do so. His every intention is to put an end to evil at the coming Day of Judgment. That's when all evildoers will stand before Him and be cast into hell.

> God has not yet *done away* *with evil, but* He clearly will *do so.*

God will destroy evil. But God doesn't have to jump every time the atheist snaps his fingers; He doesn't have to do what the atheist wants Him to do and when the atheist wants it done. But we can be assured that God will destroy evil in His own time.

THE GREATEST PROOF

The final and greatest proof of God's existence is the one Jesus alludes to in His high priestly prayer in John 17, when He says, "And this is eternal life, that they may *know* You, the only true God, and Jesus Christ whom You have sent" (verse 3).

Have you met God personally, experientially, heart to heart? Has He come to live in your life? If so, you know there's a God. You've experienced His life-transforming power in your heart.

The surest way to come to know God is through the pathway of the Cross. Jesus came to reveal God, and He comes into our lives to reveal God personally and intimately in our hearts. He's willing to come and fill the God-shaped blank in your heart as only He, the living Son of God, can do.

CONCLUSION

Years ago I saw an episode of the original TV series *Star Trek*. The story involved a Voyager spacecraft sent out from Earth through the solar system, and it had disappeared for hundreds of years. Somehow it collected unto itself all kinds of other equipment and technology and intelligence. Then it headed back to Earth, and the whole planet was in terror of this enormously powerful thing coming right at them. What was it going to do? Was it going to destroy the world?

Well, of course, Captain Kirk was dispatched to save the day. When he finally encountered this gigantic apparatus and was able to communicate with it, he found that what it wanted was not to destroy the world but to know the world's creator. It also wanted to be joined to its creator. I thought, *Wow, what a spiritual truth. That's what every human heart should desire above all else—to know God, the Creator, and be united with Him.*

Is a spacecraft more spiritual than we are? We've heard about intelligent machines and powerful machines, but that's the first time I ever heard of a spiritual machine. What a lesson for us.

Atheism: Religion of Fools

The fool has said in his heart, "There is no God."
They are corrupt, and have done abominable iniquity;
there is none who does good.

PSALM 53:1

There once was an atheist who did crow,
"There's no place above or below."
And so when he died,
The minister sighed,
"All dressed up, and no place to go!"

So goes the limerick. To some, God may seem so obscured that they even deny He exists. But as the provocative title of this chapter reflects, atheism is the religion of fools. Let's investigate that.

First of all, I believe that statement is true because God declared it, just as we have seen: "The fool has said in his heart, 'There is no God'" (Psalms 14:1; 53:1). For Christians and those who believe the Scriptures to be the Word of God, that should be completely sufficient. If God has declared it, that's it.

> God declares that those who say there is no God are fools.

God, who knows the human heart and mind, having created both, declares that those who say there is no God are fools.

EXPERIENCE DEMONSTRATES ATHEISM'S FOLLIES

Not only has God declared atheism to be folly, but experience also clearly demonstrates this.

We observed earlier how the twentieth century came to be known as the century of atheism. Never before in history had there been the number of atheists as in the twentieth century, especially in such positions of influence and power. They were the products of the great apostles of atheism who arose in the nineteenth century, men like Karl Marx, Sigmund Freud, and Friedrich Nietzsche. And the works of Charles Darwin were used mightily by atheists.

No doubt Nietzsche was the great high priest of this movement. He once said, "God is dead." Somebody quipped:

"God is dead."—*Nietzsche*
"Nietzsche is dead."—*God*

Nietzsche died in 1900, by which time he and his colaborers of atheism had brought to birth the age of atheism. What has it produced? Genocide. The twentieth century was the bloodiest on record, more barbaric on a wider scale than any other period in time.

It was the fulfillment of what an evil, atheistic character says in Dostoevsky's 1880 novel *The Brothers Karamazov:* "[E]verything is permitted…since there is no infinite God, there's no such thing as virtue either and there's no need for it at all."[1] To paraphrase, if God doesn't exist, every evil is permissible. But Christians would counter that since there *is* a God, all *good* things are permissible. What a world of difference between the two.

Historians tell us that in the twentieth century in the age of atheism, under the atheistic philosophies of Nazism and communism, one hundred fifty million people were butchered—a tragic consequence indeed. That's vastly more people than were killed in all of mankind's wars in earlier centuries.[2]

Experience demonstrates atheism's follies.

The famous twentieth-century philosopher Will Durant said something I believe should be seriously considered today by all thinking people: "The greatest question of our time is not communism vs. individualism, nor Europe vs. America, not even the East vs. the West; it is whether men can bear to live without God."[3] That's exactly what so many are trying to do in our nation today.

Those who profess themselves to be atheists make up a tiny minority of our population—about 5 or 6 percent. But there are far more practicing atheists, though they would never verbalize it. They may attend church every Sunday, but from Monday morning to Saturday night, God has no place in their thoughts. As the psalmist notes, they "do not call upon God" (53:4). There's no place for prayer in their lives. They do not seek His face and His Word. They have no devotional life. They're practical atheists.

In our society many practical atheists prefer to use an alias. What are the most popular aliases for atheists today? One would be *humanists.* The atheist says, "Down with God." The humanist says, "Up with man." They're saying the same thing; they simply emphasize different sides of the same scale.

There's also the alias of *secularists. Secularism* was the term invented in the nineteenth century by George Holyoake, the British skeptic and unbeliever. The secularists have simply ruled God out of the universe. He has been quietly dismissed not only from our schools and universities but also from every part of polite society.

Think about today's trashy television talk shows. What do they talk about? They mainstream weirdness, continually sinking deeper into the sewer to find something even more unbelievably weird than whatever they talked about in previous shows. The result is that weirdness becomes popular and imitated by other fools.

Imagine being in the studio audience for one of those programs as they're talking about incest, homosexuality, adultery, group sex, or whatever other immorality they have on the agenda that day. You hold up your hand. You're asked to stand, and the microphone is extended to you. You say, "But God has said in His Word..."

Can you hear the reaction? "Oh, wait, wait, wait. We don't talk about that sort of thing on this show. Don't you know we adhere to the strict separation of church and talk show?" What they mean is that they believe in the separation of God from human society. In their minds, God has nothing to say about this world. The result of such talk is the utter cheapening of human life to where it means nothing at all.

What are other results of atheism that confirm its folly? Just recently I saw a policeman on television say, "There are people out there today in this generation who would just as soon shoot you as look at you, without the least compunction or remorse." I heard on the news about a man who was driving down a street and stopped his car, walked up to a woman standing on the curb, and shot her four or five times. Why did he kill her? She looked at him the wrong way.

Darwin and Nietzsche in the nineteenth century pointed the way for Hitler in the twentieth century. Hitler looked to Nietzsche and to Darwin for his views. It was a small step from Nietzsche's superman to Hitler's superrace. Hitler's views led to the deaths of more than fifty million people—not just the millions of Jews whom he liquidated because he deemed them racially inferior, but millions of others around the globe who were killed as a direct result of the war that Hitler's actions started.

Ideas have consequences. Marx was midwife to Stalin and Mao Zedong, who between the two of them killed over a hundred million people. Yes indeed, the folly of an idea can destroy many.

We've heard the continuing complaint that Christianity throughout history has caused the deaths of many people. There's no doubt that thousands of people were killed in the Crusades. But the Crusades were simply an attempt to take back Jerusalem, the Holy City, from the Muslims, who had conquered it earlier. We also know that in the twentieth century, the Israelis, again by an armed attempt, took Jerusalem from the Muslims. How many times have you heard that bewailed on television? How many atheists have you heard complaining about that?

If armed Hindus came into Saudi Arabia today and took the city of Mecca away from the Muslims, would there be an outcry if the Muslims attempted to take it back? I should think practically none. Yet the cries against the Crusades are unending. I'm not an apologist for the Crusades, but I think they ought to be put into perspective. Furthermore, in the Crusades, thousands died. Under atheism, one hundred seventy million died.

Atheism not only makes life cheap, but it deprives it of any meaning or any significance. Recall the twig statement I quoted earlier from Dr. Stephen Jay Gould, professor at Harvard. He was one of the most authoritative and influential atheists of our time. He was an evolutionist and a self-confessed communist. And he declared in one of his articles that a human being is nothing more than a dead twig, like one you find in your backyard. Not a living branch cut off from the tree, and certainly not as glorious as a tree, but just a dried-up twig, good for nothing but to be put in a shredder or cast into the fire.

Does that not fill you with inspiration about how significant you are and what meaning your life has? *You twig, you!*

How different that is from what a Christian is told by Christ:

- Your life has vast significance.
- You've been adopted into the family of God and given His name.
- You've been created by the Almighty.
- You're loved by our Father in heaven.
- He has called you to a wonderful and purposeful life.
- You're to join with Him in the greatest effort in the history of mankind: to bring other people into eternal life.
- You possess an inheritance among the saints, with life in paradise forever and ever.

No wonder so many college students destroy their lives; they get tired of being a twig. Yes, atheism robs life of any meaning or purpose. If there's anything the atheist can't stand, it's the idea that we have some purpose to our lives. They say it's all simply a matter of chance and whatever looks like purpose is nothing more than chance.

ATHEISM LEADS TO BONDAGE

Atheism also deprives life of freedom. We're told that not only is there no God, but there's also no such thing as the "mind." There's just the brain, and the brain secretes thoughts like the liver secretes bile. Isn't that encouraging?

I wonder how much bile you secreted this week? Did you control it? Did you think about it? Of course not. It's absolutely natural; it's beyond your control. And so it is, the atheists say, with our thoughts. They're secreted by our brain. There is no mind; there's just this brain-bile we ooze out, which causes us to do things we have no control over. We aren't free, they say.

> *Atheists say our thoughts are secreted by our brain. There is no mind.*

Along these lines behavioral psychologist B. F. Skinner declared in his book *Beyond Freedom and Dignity* that we're biologically determined in absolutely all we do. Therefore, we have no dignity and no freedom, and we're not responsible.

This has gone so far that today we have "the victim defense," which is, "The victim made me do it. It's all the fault of that corpse I killed." Or, "My father made me do it." Or, "My mother made me do it."

It all comes down to this: "I'm not responsible. I have no freedom; therefore, I have no guilt. There's no such thing, really, as crime." After all, how could anyone be hauled into court and convicted for secreting too much bile from the liver, the brain, or wherever? Recently I read in a magazine that our criminal justice system is being overthrown by this kind of thinking that pervades the juries in America.

So what is Christianity? Is it, as atheist Richard Dawkins suggests in his best-selling book, *The God Delusion,* a "mind virus" that infects those of us naive enough to believe?[4]

ATHEISM'S TOGAS ARE RIPPED OFF

But in our age, something else is happening in regard to atheism. The togas are being ripped off the gods of atheism, and they're being revealed for what they really are. People are seeing them for the first time.

Take Nietzsche, for example. This bold conqueror who rushes out like Superman, grabs a lightning bolt, and throws it back at God. This destroyer of God who cries out at God's funeral, "God is dead!" What a mighty hero he must have been. What Promethean proportions he must have had. What a model to follow in the great march forward into humanistic atheism.

And yet, in a column by Pat Buchanan entitled "Clay-Footed Gods of Atheism," Friedrich Nietzsche is described as "a syphilitic, a homosexual."[5] Moreover, he hated women. "Woman," he said, "is by nature a snake.... Thou goest to women? Do not forget thy whip."[6]

He was also a wimp. Even Bertrand Russell, a fellow atheist, observed that Nietzsche knew that most women would have gotten the whip away from him, so Nietzsche didn't go to women; he went to men.

Nietzsche was also an anti-Semite.

Furthermore, he eventually went insane. Since the world he described is an irrational world, he obliged by leading his followers into that realm of insanity.

So there you have it: the great high priest of atheism—a syphilitic, homosexual, sexist, anti-Semitic, anti-Christian bigot, and an insane fool who said both in his heart and with his lips and pen, "There is no God."

The results of atheistic philosophies have been further exposed in Nazism and communism, and we've seen what Freud and Darwin and Marx and Nietzsche let loose upon this planet. The sight is a horrid one, to say the least.

CONCLUSION

Wonder of wonders, here in the midst of atheism we find a renaissance of belief in God.

In a chapter he calls "The God Who Would Not Die," British historian Paul Johnson says in his book *The Quest for God* (written at the end of the twentieth century): "From one perspective—the perspective of human spirituality—the most extraordinary thing about the twentieth century was the failure of God to die. The collapse of mass religious belief, especially among the educated and prosperous, had been widely and confidently predicted. It did not take place. Somehow, God survived, flourished even. At the end of the twentieth century, the idea of a personal, living God is as lively and real as ever, in the minds and hearts of countless millions of men and women throughout our planet."[7]

In fact, according to a report published by the Roper Center for Public Opinion Research at the University of Connecticut, belief in God appears to be getting stronger, based on national surveys on God, religion, and religious beliefs.[8]

Well, *mirabile dictu*, "marvelous to tell." Yes, Nietzsche is dead… but God is very much alive.

4

Is God Truly Hidden?

He has put eternity in their hearts.
ECCLESIASTES 3:11

Deep in the collective mind-set of the entire human race, there exists the awareness of God. In every culture and in all known languages, His presence is somehow manifested. We sense His majesty in the height of the mountains. We know His power in the strength of a storm. We see His artistry in the sunrise. We see His creativity in the variety of life forms that pervade our world. We see His order in the universe. We see His brilliance reflected in the diamond. We see His detailed handiwork in the simplest cell and in the vastness of space. We see His creative power in the diversity displayed in His creation and in the birth of every new creature. We hear His whispers in our hearts.

"He has also set eternity in the hearts of men" (Ecclesiastes 3:11, NIV). He breathed life into us, and we're all born in the image of God, with a divine spark. His law is written on our hearts, and our own consciences bear witness of His will.

Why, then, do we not see Him clearly? Why are we left to seek Him and wonder about Him? The longing of our souls is to talk to Him and have Him respond audibly. We just want to ask Him a few questions. We want to know Him intimately. Why does He not roll back the sky and reveal Himself?

Sensing God somewhere isn't enough for us somehow. We want a lot more. We want His visible presence, and we want His verbal approval. We want to know that all is and will be well.

In Western civilization the fingerprints of God in nature have been called "the Book of Nature"—for example, by Sir Francis Bacon, the father of the scientific method. But even though this "Book" is vast and varied, it isn't totally sufficient.

> *We were never meant to be satisfied with whatever crumbs of religion we could reason out by ourselves.*

Nor were we ever meant to be satisfied with whatever crumbs of religion we could reason out by ourselves. God has prepared a feast for us, but too many of us stay under the table eating the crumbs.

It isn't enough for us to sense a glint of God's glory in creation or feel the breath of wind stirring in our hearts. And we should never be content with "worshiping God in nature" or "living according to our conscience." It was never God's intention that this should be all and enough for us. It's only to show us God is there and to encourage us to seek Him.

And when we seek Him with all our hearts, our seeking will not be in vain.

WHEN THINGS BECOME TOPSY-TURVY

You know those little snow-globe toys we often see at Christmastime—those little worlds with water and "snow" inside? They may be scenes of a small town, a little schoolhouse, a church, or home. You can take those little plastic globes and shake them, then set them down, and all the snow will fall.

Sometimes life on earth can seem like life inside those plastic bubbles—everything topsy-turvy while someone is shaking our world. Through it all, God seems hidden.

When bad things happen to good people, some people conclude that if there's a God, He cannot be omnipotent or He cannot be good.

In reply, our argument is that there *is* a God, He *is* omnipotent, and He *is* good…but humanity is fallen. Because of our being fallen, God may seem hidden to us, but as Francis Schaeffer once stated in a book title, "He is there and He is not silent."

People in every culture have to deal with particular falsehoods that their culture may teach about God. Most of us in our culture are trained to think of a purely naturalistic world. We're taught through the theory of evolution to believe that nature has created itself and continues to correct itself. Some Christians buy into evolution, though adding the stipulation that God was the force behind evolution. But in doing so they demote God's roles as the creator and sustainer of life.

If you have a purely naturalistic view of the universe and you assume it runs itself of its own accord, God is indeed hidden to you, for the Bible teaches us that Jesus Christ sustains the universe: "In him all things hold together" (Colossians 1:17, ESV). It is He, the co-Creator, who upholds all life.

THE VALLEY OF THE BLIND

The classic short story *The Country of the Blind* from H. G. Wells is a fascinating tale about a race of people living in a large valley. A dreaded plague had descended upon the inhabitants, rendering them all blind. Even worse, the blindness was passed on to their children and grandchildren and every generation thereafter. For centuries, this entire populace had lived in perpetual darkness so that even the memory of vision had disappeared entirely.

Because their valley was surrounded by incredibly high mountains, they were cut off from the rest of the world. But at one point an intrepid explorer found his way over a high pass in the mountains. As he made his way down, his feet slipped, and he slid a long way until at last he landed unconscious on the valley floor. The hearing of the people in the valley was exceedingly acute, so they heard his landing. They walked toward the sound and found this man lying unconscious on the ground.

When they revived him, they were astounded to hear him babble about imaginary things. They assumed he must have done something to his head when he fell, for he talked about things that didn't exist, such as a blue sky and red flowers. They thought, *Blue? What's that? And red? There's no such thing.* He kept using these strange words. He talked about his eyes, his vision, and what he could see. They'd never heard of such things and had no idea what he was talking about. The man was obviously out of his mind. He was delusional.

As he talked about his eyes and what they could do, they eventually realized that this was the real source of his problem. But they graciously put up with him in spite of his continued babblings. He was their "valley idiot," but they tried to be kind to him.

Months passed, and having been taken with the beauty of the chief's daughter, at length the man fell in love with her, and she with him—though she had not the faintest idea what he meant when he said, "You're beautiful." At last he asked for her hand in marriage. But his request was denied. It just wasn't right for the chief's daughter to marry the valley idiot.

But their love was still strong. So it was decided that because the man's eyes were the cause of his problem, they would simply cut out his eyes and thus restore him to his right mind. Then he could marry the girl.

As I read this tale, to my astonishment the character actually agreed to do this. I wanted to shout to him, "No! No! The problem isn't you. It's *their* problem."

> *They decided to simply cut out his eyes.*

As the day drew nigh for the surgery on his eyes, the man was still prepared to go through with it. Finally, at the very last moment—as he lay on the operating table—he came to his senses. He jumped up, ran out, climbed the mountain, and disappeared.

As fanciful as this story is, it bears a resemblance to the world in which we live. Because of sin, the whole human race tumbled, as it were, into a valley of the blind. From the high estate we'd been given originally, we fell into a fallen state—that of the "natural" man or woman. What's our problem? Our minds are darkened, our wills corrupted. We've lost our spiritual sight and our spiritual hearing. We have eyes and see not; we have ears and hear not. In his messages, Billy Graham calls on people to "listen with the ears of their spirit." But we have lost that ability.

We were created perfect, but now a veil is over our minds so that our thinking is darkened. Our hearts have been replaced with hearts of stone, and we're at enmity with God. We're "dead in trespasses and sins" (Ephesians 2:1).

And the real tragedy is that on our own, we never realized it. Those who are still in such a state do not realize it. The Bible says, "The natural man does not receive the things of the Spirit of God, for they are foolishness to him; nor can he know them, because they are spiritually discerned" (1 Corinthians 2:14). Who is the "natural man"? He's the unregenerate man.

The natural man today looks upon those who have spiritual sight the same way the inhabitants in that valley looked upon the stranger who came to them from over the mountains. They don't want to operate on you with scalpels; since this is a spiritual matter, they'll operate on you with their pens or their tongues. They'll mock you and ridicule you. They'll say that the things you talk about don't exist and that you're delusional, just as Freud did when he said all religion is either psychosis or neurosis. There it is again: *You* have a problem; Freud didn't. The same attitude is found among most of the Christianity bashers you see on news programs and talk shows.

In this natural state, people can be winsome and appear intelligent and reasonable, but when they're confronted with Christ, the axiom proves itself: Christ is the touchstone of character. I've seen the tiger that comes out in some of these people when their need for Christ is pointed out by a devoted believer. Their claws are extended, and they show their natural animosity to God.

In the story from H. G. Wells, our friend eventually fled the valley after the inhabitants in the valley wanted to make him blind. That's still what unbelievers try to do. They work diligently on all our children, grandchildren, friends, neighbors, and co-workers to accomplish that purpose.

But we want to take away their blindness and give them sight. What an amazing difference it makes. That's the wonderful task God has given us, which is accomplished through the gospel of Jesus Christ. It's our privilege to do that.

Remember that the entire story of the Bible is about three things: generation (Creation), *de*generation (the Fall), and *re*generation (Restoration). That's the whole Bible in a nutshell.

In the early days of my ministry, a man said to me, "You shouldn't preach about being born again; it's not a Presbyterian doctrine." I had to inform him it most definitely *is* a Presbyterian doctrine, as well as a Methodist doctrine, a Baptist doctrine, an Episcopal doctrine, a Lutheran doctrine, a Catholic doctrine, and a doctrine of all Christian churches. It's usually labeled "regeneration" instead of rebirth, but it's called both in the Bible.

It's what the Bible is all about. While the first two chapters of Genesis deal with *generation* and the third chapter deals with *degeneration,* the entire rest of the Bible—the remainder of the Old Testament plus the full New Testament all the way through the end of Revelation—deals with *regeneration.*

Regeneration is the essence of Christianity. Christ said, "Behold, I make all things new" (Revelation 21:5). He raises people from the dead—not only physically, but spiritually as well. He gives life to the dead, sight to the blind, hearing to the deaf.

Regeneration is the essence of Christianity.

So we recognize this marked difference: There's the natural man, who's degenerate, depraved, sinful, lost, blind, deaf, and dead, whose heart is a stone, who's at enmity with God. And there are those who have been born again, who are changed by the Spirit of God and made new.

Our vision is limited. God's vision is not.

On one occasion coauthor Jerry Newcombe was on a radio talk show with a very liberal host. During a commercial break, she lit up a cigarette and said to him, "Jesus Shmesus. He means absolutely nothing to me."

Jerry said to her, "Sandy, if your eyes were truly open, you would see that every beat of your heart is by the grace of Jesus Christ."

His remark offended her greatly. When the break was over and they returned live on the air, she brought up this little exchange. As could be expected on a liberal show like that, the callers took

Sandy's side. So many people are blind to the truth. And that's why God seems hidden to them.

He Came to His Own

C. S. Lewis pointed out that Christianity is the tale of how the real king of the universe came to earth in disguise.[1] He isn't recognized. John tells us, "He came unto his own, and his own received him not" (John 1:11, KJV). I used to think "his own" meant the Jews. While their rejection of Christ is certainly a theme of the book of John, the immediate context of John 1 implies so much more. The second person of the Trinity has entered into His own creation, but His own have not received Him. In a sense, the hidden God remained hidden to some even when He was right in front of them.

When Jesus Christ raised Lazarus from the dead after he had lain in the tomb for four days, many believed. However, some went and told the Pharisees, who then plotted to kill Jesus as well as Lazarus. Ultimately they wanted to make sure God remained hidden.

But just because human beings perceive God as hidden doesn't make Him so.

Think about those who are deceived into unbelief. Think about those who reject God, despite the witness of creation. They reject Christ, despite the witness of His resurrection. They reject the Spirit, even if He tugs at their hearts. Then they turn around and wonder, *Where is God?*

This reminds me of what Jeremiah the prophet had to deal with. He declared how the people were apostate from God. They actively worshiped other gods; they actively defied God's law, even though they'd received the unique revelation from God. Then when His inevitable judgment came, they wondered where God was. Jeremiah's response was essentially this: "Let the idols you worship come and save you" (see 2:28).

CONCLUSION

The Bible tells us, "A man's own folly ruins his life, yet his heart rages against the LORD" (Proverbs 19:3, NIV).

God is never really hidden, but tragically, from our perspective, it seems that way. Our sin makes God seem hidden. Just because a blind man doesn't see something doesn't mean it isn't there. The problem rests not with God, but with our vision.

PART II

GOD REVEALED
IN HIS SON

5

Jesus: The Great "I AM"

*Jesus said to them, "Most assuredly, I say to you,
before Abraham was, I AM."*

JOHN 8:58

The Beatific Vision...have you heard of it? It was the great quest, the be-all and end-all for many of the medieval saints of God. This Beatific Vision—the blessed vision—was a vision of God that many sought most diligently.

TO SEE GOD—THE SECRET OF SPIRITUAL RENEWAL

To see God has been the heart cry of millions down through the centuries. In the oldest book in the Bible, Job cried, "Oh, that I knew where I might find Him" (Job 23:3). The disciples of Jesus said to Him, "Lord, show us the Father, and it is sufficient for us" (John 14:8).

Yet God dwells in light inaccessible. He's the Invisible One. He's the One upon whose face no person may look and live.

Yet Moses found Him, in a certain way. He discovered Him in a bush on the side of a mountain. He was tending the sheep that belonged to his father-in-law, Jethro, and had come to the backside of the desert, to Mount Horeb, the mountain of God, where later the Ten Commandments would be given. There, on that mountainside, he saw a strange sight: a bush that burned, yet it wasn't consumed. Moses said, "I will now turn aside and see this great sight, why the bush does not burn" (Exodus 3:3).

With his staff in hand, he began to climb the mountain toward this unusual sight. As he drew closer, a voice spoke from the bush. "Do not draw near this place. Take your sandals off your feet, for the place where you stand is holy ground" (Exodus 3:5). There, from the voice in the bush, Moses received his commission to return to Egypt, where Pharaoh had sought his life, and to deliver the children of Israel from their bondage.

Then Moses asked a question that would elicit one of the greatest revelations mankind has ever known about God:

> "Indeed, when I come to the children of Israel and say to them, 'The God of your fathers has sent me to you,' and they say to me, 'What is His name?' what shall I say to them?"
>
> And God said to Moses, "I AM WHO I AM." And He said, "Thus you shall say to the children of Israel, 'I AM has sent me to you.' "
>
> Moreover God said to Moses, "Thus you shall say to the children of Israel: 'The LORD God of your fathers, the God of Abraham, the God of Isaac, and the God of Jacob, has sent me to you. This is My name forever, and this is My memorial to all generations.' " (Exodus 3:13–15)

Here we have the great revelation of the name of God. In Hebrew, the relative pronoun that separates the two names can be translated in a variety of ways. It can be "I am *who* I am" or "I am *that* I am" or "I am *because* I am" or "I am *what* I am." Here is the great incomprehensible God revealing Himself to Moses.

To see God, to meet God, to experience God is the source of spiritual life. And for those who have already met Him, it's the source of continued spiritual renewal and revival. To see God is the meaning of revival.

To experience God is the source of spiritual life.

Renewal and revival among God's people can be obtained only when we see God—when we see Him as He has shown Himself to be in His Word.

At a later time (in Exodus 33), Moses asked God to show him His glory. Moses was hidden in a cleft in the rock, and he saw God from behind as He passed by. That's all God allowed Moses to see.

Eventually God did answer Moses's request in full, but it took fourteen hundred years for his prayer to be answered. On the Mount of Transfiguration, Moses finally got to see God's glory in the face of Jesus Christ, for "His face shone like the sun" (Matthew 17:2). Here was *the* revelation; here was the true Beatific Vision. Two Old Testament saints, Moses and Elijah, along with three of the apostles, Peter, James, and John, were selected to see the ultimate glory of God revealed in Christ Jesus.

GOD CAN BE SEEN ONLY
IN THE FACE OF JESUS CHRIST

God revealed not merely His name but the express image of His person in His Son, Jesus Christ. When Philip said to Jesus, "Lord, show us the Father, and it is sufficient for us," Jesus replied, "He who has seen *Me* has seen the Father" (John 14:8–9).

The God who dwelt forever in light inaccessible had revealed Himself in the darkness of night in a stable. And He revealed His brilliant light even more clearly when midnight darkness came at noon over Golgotha as God the Son gave His life for the sin of the world.

People were always filled with wonder and awe by Jesus and His remarkable sayings and actions. When Jesus rebuked the wind and calmed the sea, the disciples said, "Who can this be, that even the winds and the sea obey Him?" (Matthew 8:27). It was His deity that inspired such awe.

In John 8, we read one of Jesus's most astonishing statements. He was engaged in a controversy with the Jews, and He was saying that they belonged to their father, the devil. They refused to accept His word; they could not accept it because they were dead in their sins. Then Jesus said, "Most assuredly, I say to you, if anyone keeps My word he shall never see death" (John 8:51).

This was more than those Jews could take. They said, "Now we know that You have a demon! Abraham is dead, and the prophets; and You say, 'If anyone keeps My word he shall never taste death.' Are You greater than our father Abraham, who is dead? And the prophets are dead. Who do You make Yourself out to be?" (8:52–53).

Jesus responded, "Your father Abraham rejoiced to see My day, and he saw it and was glad" (8:56).

The Jews in Jesus's day knew exactly what He meant.

Further astounded, they said to Him, "You are not yet fifty years old, and have You seen Abraham?" (8:57).

Then, from Jesus, came the most incredible statement of all: "Most assuredly, I say to you, before Abraham was, I AM" (8:58).

Many of us today do not grasp the full impact of these words in

John 8, but the Jews in Jesus's day knew exactly what He meant. "Then they took up stones to throw at Him" (8:59). They wanted to execute Him for blasphemy, for He, a man, spoke of Himself as God.

"Before Abraham was, I AM." The grammar of that verse should grab our attention. If He were saying He had been alive before Abraham lived on the earth, we assume He would have said, "Before Abraham was, *I was.*" Would that not be correct? Just as I could say to you (if you're younger than I am), "Before *you* were, *I* was." But Jesus said, "Before Abraham was, I AM." Or, in essence, "Even before Abraham came to be, *I always exist.*"

Repeatedly Jesus took this title of the great "I AM" upon His own lips. Earlier in John 8 He had said, "For if you do not believe that *I am He,* you will die in your sins" (verse 24). But the word "He" is not actually in the Greek text. Jesus literally said, "For if you do not believe that *I am,* you will die in your sins."

Again, that's rather strange. Here is Jesus, in person, talking to the Jews. They can hear His voice; they can see Him; they can touch Him. Obviously, He *is.* He's right there. Does it not seem strange that He would say, "Believe that I am"? In the normal sense, of course it was true. Anybody could see that. But He meant something more. And once again the Jews—being quite familiar with the Exodus passage and the divine name God had revealed to Moses—knew what Jesus meant: "For if you do not believe that I AM—that *I am God*— you will die in your sins."

We see this same "I AM" construction in John 18, when the temple police came to capture Jesus in the Garden of Gethsemane the night before His crucifixion.

Jesus therefore…went forward and said to them, "Whom are you seeking?" They answered Him, "Jesus of Nazareth." Jesus said to them, *"I am He."* …Now when He said to them, *"I am He,"* they drew back and fell to the ground. (verses 4–6)

Jesus was showing that He wasn't being overwhelmed by military power and might and that He was more than capable of destroying all these with a word.

However, He allowed Himself to be taken. As He Himself had said earlier about His life,

No one takes it from Me, but I lay it down of Myself. I have power to lay it down, and I have power to take it again. This command I have received from My Father. (John 10:18)

Later, when Jesus stood on trial before the Sanhedrin, He used the "I AM" phrase again, once more eliciting indignation from the Jews:

Again the high priest asked Him, saying to Him, "Are You the Christ, the Son of the Blessed?" Jesus said, *"I am.* And you will see the Son of Man sitting at the right hand of the Power, and coming with the clouds of heaven." Then the high priest tore his clothes and said, "What further need do we have of witnesses? You have heard the blasphemy! What do you think?" And they all condemned Him to be deserving of death. (Mark 14:61–64)

Jesus made it plain that the great "I AM" who spoke to Moses on the Mount of God was the great "I AM" who was speaking to them and who soon would be hung on an even holier mount, the mount of Calvary.

Spiritual life and renewal come from seeing God, and we can see God only in the face of Jesus Christ, the express image of the Father. In Christ, the "hidden God" is not so hidden.

THE INCREDIBLE CLAIMS OF CHRIST

Jesus Christ made incredible claims about Himself. He said, "I am the way, the truth, and the life. No one comes to the Father except through Me" (John 14:6).

If I'd been making up a religion, I probably never would have said such a thing. But Jesus had the temerity to say it. In fact, He said some of the most astonishing, amazing, unbelievable things:

I am the door. If anyone enters by Me, he will be saved. (John 10:9)

I am the resurrection and the life. (John 11:25)

I am He who lives, and was dead, and behold, *I am* alive forevermore. (Revelation 1:18)

Before Abraham was, *I AM.* (John 8:58)

He who has seen Me has seen the Father. (John 14:9)

When Christ says, "I am the way... No one comes to the Father except through Me," many people have difficulty with that statement because they simply don't understand who Jesus is. They suppose Him to be just another prophet, just another religious founder, just another great teacher, just another good man.

Of course, Jesus *was* a great prophet, a good man, a great teacher, but He was—and is—infinitely more. He sustains our very existence. Should Christ blink, so to speak, the whole universe would blink out of existence. It was made by Him, it is sustained by Him, and He controls it. He has no peer.

All of history's religious leaders were merely mortals. They've all died and rotted. But Christ is alive forevermore. Because people don't understand who Jesus Christ is, they think Christianity is just one of many religions on this earth, but it isn't so. What they need is not merely head knowledge about Jesus. They need to see how He reveals the hidden God in our own experiences, especially at our times of greatest need.

ONLY THROUGH THE EYES OF NEED

We can see Christ only through the eyes of need. We don't find Him through intellectual pursuits, through philosophic contemplation, or through linguistic analysis. As we look at Him through the prism of our tears, we see Christ in all His glory. The pure white light of Christ breaks out into all the colors of the rainbow, each tint meeting a specific need of our hearts.

Jesus reveals the hidden God in our own experiences.

Notice that "I am" is really a sentence without a predicate. I am...*what*? "I AM THAT I AM" is simply a closed loop that could go on and on: *I am that I am that I am that I am...*

Roy and Revel Hession explain this further:

The name "Jehovah" is really like a blank cheque. Your faith can fill in what He is to be to you—just what you need, as each need arises. It is not you, moreover, who are beseeching Him for this privilege, but He who is pressing it upon you. He is asking you to ask. "Hitherto have ye asked nothing in My name: ask, and ye shall receive, that your joy may be full" (John 16:24). Just as water is ever seeking the lowest depths...so is Jehovah ever seeking out man's need in order to satisfy it. Where there is need, there is God. Where there is sorrow, misery, unhappiness, suffering, confusion, folly, oppression, there is the I AM, yearning to turn man's sorrow into bliss whenever man will let Him. It is not, therefore, the hungry seeking for bread, but the Bread seeking the hungry; not the sad seeking for joy, but rather Joy seeking the sad; not emptiness seeking fulness, but rather Fulness seeking emptiness. And it is not merely that He supplies our need, but He becomes Himself the fulfilment of our need. He is ever "I am that which My people need."[1]

I remember going scuba diving for the first time when I came to Fort Lauderdale about fifty years ago. It was a fairly new sport back then, and there was little training available for it. We went out fifteen miles from Miami, they put the equipment on me, and I just jumped off the boat. There was no one swimming with me, no buddy system.

The water was crystal clear, which you couldn't tell from the boat because the wind caused quite a chop on the surface. I was in sixty feet of water, and beneath me was a vast reef. I put on my mask, stuck my head into the water, and suddenly the ocean disappeared. I found myself hovering six stories in the "air" and feeling like I was falling onto the rocks below. I tried to grab the surface of the water with my arms—it was pure instinct. I then came to my senses, realizing the water had "disappeared" only because of my face mask. Actually I had sixty feet of water between me and the rocks below. What an incredible revelation of something totally unseen, something that couldn't be seen from the boat at all.

It was like that on the fateful night when I finished reading *The Greatest Story Ever Told*. For the first time in my life, I looked up through the prism of the tears in my eyes, through the realization of my need, of my uncleanness, of my sin, of my iniquity, and I saw this One hanging upon the cross of Calvary. And I *knew*. I saw my Savior bleeding for me, and He became all that I needed, in my very needy condition:

Unclean? No longer. He cleansed me with His precious blood.

Without hope? No longer. He gave me His everlasting hope.

Unrighteous? No longer. *He* became my righteousness.

JEHOVAH—BECOMING WHAT WE NEED

There is a series of passages in the Old Testament, often called the "Jehovah texts," where we see that Jehovah *becomes* something for His people. The first of these that I discovered—in Jeremiah 23:6—was where the Lord is called Jehovah-*Tsidkenu,* which means "*I am* your righteousness."

The other Jehovah texts present the Lord in these ways:

- Jehovah-*Shalom* (Judges 6:24)—"*I am* your peace."
- Jehovah-*Ra-ah* (Psalm 23:1)—"*I am* your shepherd."
- Jehovah-*Shammah* (Ezekiel 48:35)—"*I am* the One who is there." (Wherever you are, whatever you need, He is there.)
- Jehovah-*Rapha* (Exodus 15:26)—"*I am* the One who heals."

- Jehovah-*Jireh* (Genesis 22:14)—"*I am* the One who provides." (Whatever your need may be, Jehovah Himself will become your provision.)
- Jehovah-*Nissi* (Exodus 17:15)—"*I am* your banner."

In the New Testament there are numerous places where these Old Testament phrases are echoed, identifying Jesus as Jehovah. He is truly Jehovah Jesus—our Righteousness, our Peace, our Shepherd, the One who is there, our Healer, our Provider, and our Banner.

We will know continued spiritual renewal and revival when we see Jesus as the answer to our every need, because He provides that which His people need. He is our Everything.

CONCLUSION

God is not hidden. He is revealed in Christ. Meanwhile, our suffering and our needs draw us to Jesus. We see Christ through the tears of our eyes, through the brokenness of our hearts. He's our Savior, our Redeemer, our Sanctifier, our Righteousness, our Wisdom, our Everything.

We're needy creatures, knowing we can see Christ only through a broken heart. He has said in His Word that if we ever truly seek Him, we shall see Him. One of God's great delights is to meet us at the point of our greatest need.

6

God Revealed
in Christ

No one has seen God at any time.
The only begotten Son, who is in the bosom of the Father,
He has declared Him.

JOHN 1:18

C hildren enjoy playing hide-and-seek. Some people feel God
is playing that game as well, that He's coy with them, as if
He's purposefully hiding His face from them.

But how can God be hidden when He has so clearly revealed
Himself by becoming a human being in Christ? What more could
He do?

God is *not* hidden. Once we see Jesus Christ, we realize God is anything but hidden. C. S. Lewis put it so well when he declared, "The
Son of God became a man to enable men to become sons of God."[1]

In Jesus Christ, God Himself has entered our world and has
shown us what He is like. God has made Himself known so all
humanity can know Him. He has shown Himself clearly. If unbelief
hides Him, that's the unbeliever's problem.

Jesus Christ is the divine, inescapable imperative. He's the One
before whom we'll all stand and give account.

Recently, coauthor Jerry Newcombe received an interesting insight about the supremacy of Jesus:

> I was reading a book about the faith of the presidents, and I remember, as I read through the section on John Adams, our second president, who was an extraordinary Founding Father, I was saddened to see the gradual drift in his life from a high view of Jesus to a low view. By the end of his life, Adams had essentially embraced a Unitarian view of Jesus, not a Trinitarian view. But then this thought dawned on me: Jesus Christ does not need to justify Himself before John Adams. John Adams will need to justify himself before Jesus Christ! Jesus is our judge; we are not His judge.

To say God is hidden is to deny the Christian faith.

WHY DID HE COME?

Why did Jesus come? That's a good question.

The story has oft been told of a man who accidentally kicked an anthill. When he looked down and saw all the little ants scurrying frantically around, he wanted to bend down and say to them, "Oh, I'm sorry. I didn't mean to destroy your house." He wondered how he could communicate with them. They couldn't understand anything he said. He couldn't write them a letter and stick it in the sand next to the anthill. He couldn't get a megaphone and shout to them. What could he do?

That whole ant story is errant nonsense.

It dawned on him that the only way one could communicate with ants was to *become* an ant.

And that, the story goes, is why Jesus became a man.

Nonsense. That whole story is errant nonsense.

First of all, God didn't destroy our home; we destroyed this world by our sin.

Second, God didn't have to become a human to communicate with us. The entire Old Testament is a communication from God to humanity. God spoke to us through the prophets, Scripture says. Not only that, He spoke physically and audibly to people (for example, to Moses and the people of Israel at Mount Sinai). We're intelligent creatures, not ants. We're made in the image of God. We can understand Him. God didn't have to become a man simply to bring us a message. He came for a much higher purpose—our redemption.

What Jesus Did Not Do

We think about all the good things Jesus Christ did, but it's fascinating sometimes to consider the things He did *not* do.

For example, Christ taught us in the Lord's Prayer that we should ask forgiveness every day: "Forgive us our debts, as we forgive our debtors" (Matthew 6:12). Jesus Himself never asked forgiveness for sin.

It has been said that the greatest of saints are those who see themselves to be most defiled and covered with sin. As you look in the Bible, consider Job, Isaiah, or Peter. All of them said, in effect, "Lord, I am an unclean man. Depart from me. I'm a sinner." The apostle Paul said, "Christ Jesus came into the world to save sinners, of whom I am chief" (1 Timothy 1:15).

But Jesus, the greatest saint who ever lived, was totally free from any fault or sin. He could ask, "Which of you convicts Me of sin?" (John 8:46) and know that no one could convict Him. Why? Because He was sinless. When the lives of all the other great people of history are examined, we see their feet of clay. But the closest, most minute inspection of the life of Christ reveals not a single flaw.

Even Judas, after he betrayed Christ, said, "I have sinned by betraying innocent blood" (Matthew 27:4). Pontius Pilate, who condemned Christ, said, "I find no fault in this Man" (Luke 23:4). The centurion who saw Jesus nailed to the cross said, "Certainly this was a righteous Man!" (Luke 23:47). One of the thieves who died next to Him said, "We receive the due reward of our deeds; but this Man has done nothing wrong" (Luke 23:41).

History has joined the chorus: "This is the crystal Christ; the paragon of virtue." He never asked forgiveness; He never apologized to anyone on earth; He never needed to.

Jesus never sought human counsel or asked for prayer.

I once had a couple in my office who were arguing terribly. I said to them, "One of you needs to start this off by apologizing." (Of course, they *both* needed to do it.) Then I added, "And I can tell which one is going to apologize first." They looked a little surprised. I continued, "The bigger of the two."

That's always the case with us. But Jesus was the greatest soul who ever lived, yet He never apologized. Why? Because He had nothing to apologize for.

Jesus never sought human counsel. When Nicodemus, one of the counselors of the Jews, came to see Him, Jesus didn't take the opportunity to seek counsel; rather, He gave counsel to Nicodemus. The Jews wondered, "Where then did this Man get all these things?" (Matthew 13:56). They also asked, "How does this Man know letters, having never studied?" (John 7:15). Jesus never went to school in the sense we know. He never studied. Yet His knowledge was in no way lacking.

Jesus never corrected His teachings. Most people who write a textbook soon have to write a second edition, amend it, change it, and then change it again. A few years later it's completely out of date, and the whole thing is worthless. Jesus never did any of that. Nor have the centuries proved His teachings to be out-of-date in any way.

Jesus never asked for prayer. You say, "Well, what about in the Garden of Gethsemane? Didn't He ask the three disciples with Him to pray for Him?" No, He said, "Watch and pray, lest you enter into temptation" (Mark 14:38). I've asked my congregation to pray for me many times. But Jesus never asked for prayer.

We all seek the sympathetic ear, we desire the sympathetic heart, and we want people to commiserate with our problems. Which of us has ever known trouble like Christ knew? Jesus suffered as no other man has ever suffered, yet He never sought sympathy.

He refused sympathy when it was offered Him. As He was dragging His cross up the Via Dolorosa, the women of Jerusalem wept over Him, and He said to them, "Daughters of Jerusalem, do not weep for Me, but weep for yourselves and for your children.... For if they do these things in the green wood, what will be done in the dry?" (Luke 23:28, 31).

Jesus was unique. There never has been anyone like Him. This sinless One offers to clothe us with His perfection. He came to bring reconciliation between humanity and God.

FULLY HUMAN

The great confession of the Christian church is that Jesus of Nazareth is Jehovah of hosts. He's the second person of the triune God: Father, Son, and Holy Spirit. Jesus is fully God, yet fully man. When we confess our belief in Jesus, we're confessing that He was a man—and fully a man. Not many today deny that.

In the early centuries of the church, the Docetists (their name came from the Greek word *dokeo*, which means "to seem") argued that Jesus only *seemed* to be a man. He was actually a phantasm, they said, and not a man at all.

But Jesus was fully human in every way. His ancestry was obviously human. Jesus was born of the Virgin Mary (Matthew 1:18–25; Luke 1:30–35). He was the descendant of David (Matthew 1:1; Luke 1:31–32) as well as of Adam (Luke 3:23–38). He even had half brothers and half sisters (Matthew 13:55–56). He had a human ancestry and human blood relations, at least on His mother's side.

He also had a human appearance. There was nothing about Him to cause people to think He was anything other than a man. As someone once said, "The veil that Godhead wore shut out more glory than we could bear," but He was looked upon as a man by His friends and His enemies as well. "Is this not the carpenter's son?" they said (Matthew 13:55).

People thought Him a man even after His resurrection. Mary mistook Him for the gardener. The disciples on the road to Emmaus thought He was an ordinary stranger who was surprisingly ignorant of the great events that had just transpired in their community. He appeared to be a man. And He claimed to be a man—even to be the Son of Man.

GOD BECOMES MAN

We believe in Jesus Christ—not merely Jesus, but Jesus Christ. *Christ*, the Greek word for *messiah*, means "the anointed one." In the Old Testament, prophets were anointed, priests were anointed, and kings were anointed; likewise Jesus is the anointed Prophet, Priest, and King, the Divine Redeemer, the Messiah of God.

The title of *Christ* points to His deity and reminds us that Jesus was not merely human but also divine. He was the God-man *(theanthropos)*—not a man who became God, but God who became flesh and dwelt among us.

If Jesus were not God, He couldn't be our Redeemer. Scripture makes it plain that no *man* can redeem his brother. The sufferings of Christ would not have been sufficient to pay for the sins of the world were those sufferings not infinite in value. Because Jesus was divine, He was the great divine Redeemer.

> *If Jesus were not God, He couldn't be our Redeemer.*

All the big guns of the skeptics and atheists down through the centuries have been aimed at His divinity, and all the unbelievers have denied it. All the cults today—whether Jehovah's Witnesses, Mormons, Christian Scientists, or others—deny the unique deity of Jesus Christ. They deny the basic, foundational tenet of the Christian faith, the rock upon which all of Christianity stands: Jesus Christ is the unique God-man come in the flesh.

The Bible makes it clear that Jesus exercises the attributes of deity.

He has *omnipotence.* Jesus declared, "*All authority* has been given to Me in heaven and on earth" (Matthew 28:18). He not only claimed this power and authority but demonstrated it frequently during His time on earth:

- He demonstrated His power over nature. He stilled the winds and silenced the waves. He walked upon the sea. (See Mark 4:39; Matthew 14:26.)
- He demonstrated His omnipotent power over the devil and his demons. Jesus said, " 'Away with you, Satan!'… Then the devil left Him" (Matthew 4:10–11). At His command, demons departed in obedience. (See Luke 8:26–33.)

- He demonstrated His power over the very angels of heaven and referred to them—amazingly, if you think about it—as *His* angels. (See Matthew 13:41; 24:31.)
- He demonstrated His power over disease. All manner of it fled before His touch. (See Luke 4:38–39; 5:12–13; 8:42–48.)
- Finally, He even demonstrated His power over death. Having raised others in His lifetime, He raised Himself by His own power and demonstrated the divine attribute of omnipotence. (See Luke 8:40–42, 49–55; John 11:1–44.)

Jesus also demonstrated the attribute of *omniscience*. John's gospel notes this response of Jesus to the crowds: "Jesus did not commit Himself to them, because He knew all men, and had no need that anyone should testify of man, for He knew what was in man" (John 2:24–25).

He also had the attribute of *omnipresence*. After giving His followers the Great Commission to go into all the world and preach the gospel, the very next thing Jesus said was this: "And lo, I am with you always" (Matthew 28:20). His disciples have gone out, first by the dozens and scores, and then by the hundreds and thousands and tens of thousands. They've gone into every continent, every nation, every tribe, and every tongue upon the face of the earth. They've crossed the hottest deserts and plunged through the thickest jungles and scaled the highest mountains. And wherever they've gone, on land or sea, *Jesus has always been with each one of them.* He is omnipresent.

> *Wherever His disciples have gone, Jesus has always been with each one. He is omnipresent.*

CONCLUSION

A contemporary Jew has said this about Jesus:

> The significant fact is that time has not faded the vividness of
> his image. Poetry still sings his praise. No Moslem ever sings,
> "Mohammed, lover of my soul," nor does any Jew say of
> Moses the Teacher, "I need thee every hour."[2]

Jesus alone is the lover of our souls and the One whom we need
every hour as Savior and Lord of our lives. May we all learn, even
now, to bow the knee and confess Him as our all in all, the King of
our hearts and souls, and sing with the hymnist:

> All hail the power of Jesus' Name!
> Let angels prostrate fall;
> Bring forth the royal diadem,
> And crown Him Lord of all.[3]

As the fourth-century Nicene Creed puts it:

> We believe in one Lord, Jesus Christ, the only Son of God,
> eternally begotten of the Father, God from God, Light from
> Light, true God from true God, begotten, not made, one in
> Being with the Father. Through him all things were made.[4]

Amen.

How I Know
Jesus Is God

When Jesus came into the region of Caesarea Philippi,
He asked His disciples, saying, "Who do men say that I,
the Son of Man, am?" So they said, "Some say John the Baptist,
some Elijah, and others Jeremiah or one of the prophets."
He said to them, "But who do you say that I am?"
Simon Peter answered and said, "You are the Christ,
the Son of the living God." Jesus answered and said to him,
"Blessed are you, Simon Bar-Jonah, for flesh and blood has not
revealed this to you, but My Father who is in heaven."

MATTHEW 16:13–17

Jesus Christ asked His disciples this question: "Who do men say that I am?"

George Gallup answered it for us in a Gallup Poll some years ago, with his findings published under the title "How America Sees Jesus." The poll revealed that 81 percent of Americans profess themselves to be Christians, 5 percent profess to be atheists, and 2 percent to be Jews (plus a few assorted others).

Another poll showed 80 percent of Americans believe Jesus was the Son of God, but only 42 percent said they believed He was God among men.[1] Now that's a tremendous discrepancy. Though I've repeatedly seen this incongruity in the minds of people I've talked with, here it was confirmed by a national survey.

What Is Meant by "Son of God"?

Who is Jesus Christ? Next to the question of whether there's a God, this is no doubt the most important question that can be urged upon the human mind. Jesus asked, "Who do you say that I am?" Who is this One upon whom our hopes of heaven depend? Who is Jesus? What is meant by the biblical term "Son of God"?

In the rather irreverent motion picture *Oh, God!* the God character is asked the question, "Is Jesus your son?" The cigar-smoking God replies, "Yes, he's my son, and so is Buddha, and so is Muhammad, et cetera."

So what does it really mean that Jesus is the Son of God? Is that something different than the fact that He Himself is God? Who is this Jesus of Nazareth?

I've asked many people the question "Who do you think Jesus Christ is?" I've received many answers. Some say He was just a man. Others say He was the Son of God. Probing their answers a bit to see if they understood what they were saying or if the words were merely clichés, I responded, "Well, I'm a son of God. Is He any different from me?" (Of course, there's an infinite gulf between us, but I was trying to get them to think.)

Jesus also frequently called Himself the "Son of Man," a Messianic title taken from an Old Testament passage in the book of Daniel that speaks volumes about the uniqueness of Jesus Christ:

I was watching in the night visions,
And behold, One like the Son of Man,
Coming with the clouds of heaven!
He came to the Ancient of Days,
And they brought Him near before Him.
Then to Him was given dominion and glory and a
    kingdom,
That all peoples, nations, and languages should serve
    Him.
His dominion is an everlasting dominion,
Which shall not pass away,
And His kingdom the one
Which shall not be destroyed. (Daniel 7:13–14)

So we see Jesus was the Son of Man, but what did He mean by "Son of God"?

Whereas millions of Americans seem quite perplexed and confused about this, the Jews in Jesus's day had no difficulty understanding it. When He spoke of God as His Father, they became so enraged they took up rocks to stone Him. When He asked why, they answered, "For blasphemy, and because You, being a Man, make Yourself God" (John 10:33). To paraphrase: "By calling God Your Father, You're making Yourself equal with God." And the Jews understood well what that meant.

During a conversation with a gentleman who thought Jesus was just a man like anyone else, I said, "I think I have some startling and astonishing news for you. According to the Bible and the historic Christian faith, Jesus of Nazareth was and is the infinite, eternal Creator of the universe, the Almighty God."

Instantly his eyes filled with tears, and he said to me, "I've never heard that before, and yet I've always thought that's the way it ought to be."

That's precisely the way it *is*. Jesus Christ *is* God—not a mere created being. The Trinity does not consist of Father, Holy Spirit, and creature but of God the Father, God the Son, and God the Holy Spirit.

The fact that Jesus Christ is God incarnate—God in human flesh—is the most basic, most important, most distinctive teaching of the Christian faith. Only Jesus claimed to be divine, and only Christianity claims that its Founder is divine. Moses made no such claim, nor Buddha, nor Muhammad, nor Lao-tzu, nor Confucius, nor any other religious teacher. Only Jesus made that claim. And it created chaos among the Jews of Palestine.

Many people today think that the essence of Christianity is the teachings of Jesus. That isn't so. The teachings of Jesus are somewhat secondary to Christianity. If you read the epistles of the apostle Paul, which make up about half of the New Testament, you'll see almost nothing whatsoever said about the teachings of Jesus. Not one of His parables is mentioned. In fact, throughout the rest of the New Testament, there's little reference to the teachings of Jesus.

The teachings of Jesus are secondary to Christianity.

In the Apostles' Creed, the most universally held Christian creed, there's no reference to the teachings of Jesus or to the example of Jesus. In fact, in recounting Christ's earthly life, the creed states simply that He was "born of the Virgin Mary, suffered under Pontius Pilate, was crucified, dead, and was buried." It mentions only two days in Jesus's life—that of His birth and that of His death.

Christianity centers not in the teachings of Jesus but in the person of Jesus as the incarnate God who came into this world to take upon Himself our guilt and to die in our place.

We in the ministry are repeatedly told in seminary that we're not to preach ourselves and that a significant flaw in any minister's preaching is the continual preaching of self. That's considered totally out of place in the pulpit. Yet Jesus Christ, the Master Preacher, the Great Exemplar, constantly preached about Himself: "I am the good shepherd... I am the way... I am the truth... I am the light... I am the door." *I, I, I.* Christ was always preaching Himself, because it's in the person of Christ that our hope of salvation is found.

Was Jesus a Good Man?

Many people say Jesus was a good man. But do you remember when somebody came to Him and said, "Good Teacher," and He replied, in effect, "Stop right there. Why do you call Me good?" Jesus had just been teaching that all people were sinful. Then someone comes and calls Him "good." Jesus said, "Why do you call Me good? No one is good but One, that is, God" (Luke 18:18–19).

So you see, He hung up his questioner on the horns of a dilemma. If Jesus were merely a man, He was not good, for He had just been teaching that all people were sinful. If Jesus was good, then He was God, because He'd just gotten through teaching that there's only One who is good, and that is God. If Jesus is good, He is God; if Jesus isn't God, He isn't good.

C. S. Lewis puts this dilemma in memorable language:

I am trying here to prevent anyone saying the really foolish thing that people often say about Him: "I'm ready to accept Jesus as a great moral teacher, but I don't accept His claim to be God." That is the one thing we must not say. A man who was merely a man and said the sort of things Jesus said would not be a great moral teacher. He would either be a lunatic—on a level with the man who says he is a poached egg—or else he would be the Devil of Hell. You must make your choice. Either this man was, and is, the Son of God: or else a madman or something worse. You can shut Him up for a fool, you can spit at Him and kill Him as a demon; or you can fall at His feet and call Him Lord and God. But let us not come with any patronising nonsense about His being a great human teacher. He has not left that open to us. He did not intend to.[2]

Jesus was either God, or He was an evil man. He said He was the only way to heaven and all who trusted in Him would be everlastingly saved. If anybody denied Him, that person would be denied before the Father and would be shut out from paradise. Based upon those teachings, countless millions of people suffered the agonies of the arena. They were covered with tar and lighted as torches for Nero's garden. They were placed in sacks with vipers. They were thrown to the lions. They were killed by whatever means the depravity of mankind could invent, both in the past and at the present.

If Jesus was not all He claimed, then He was a great demon or the arch-deceiver of all times. But His church, in all its branches—all historic Christian denominations—has held that Jesus Christ was 100 percent divine and 100 percent human. He was God, and He was a man. He was the theanthropos, the God-man. All true Christian churches have held this belief.

WHAT DO THE HISTORIC CREEDS SAY?

The great creeds of the church have also affirmed that Christ was God.

- Church leaders from all over the known world came together at the Council of Nicaea (a suburb of Constantinople) in AD 325, the first and greatest of the ecumenical councils. After many months they wrote what became known as the Nicene Creed, including these lines: "We believe in one Lord, Jesus Christ, the only son of God, eternally begotten of the Father, God from God, Light from Light, true God from true God, begotten, not made."

- The Council of Chalcedon (in 451) stated this: "We unite in teaching all men to confess the one and only Son, our Lord Jesus Christ. This selfsame one is perfect both in deity and in humanness."

- The Augsburg Confession (1530) of the Lutheran Church says this: "the Son of God, did assume the human nature in the womb of the blessed Virgin Mary, so that there are two natures, the divine and the human, inseparably enjoined in one Person, one Christ, true God and true man."

- In the sixteenth century, the Thirty-Nine Articles of Religion of the Church of England articulated the core doctrines of the Anglican Church, including this affirmation: "The Son, which is the Word of the Father, begotten from everlasting of the Father, the very [*very* means 'true'] and eternal God, and of one substance with the Father, took Man's nature in the womb of the blessed Virgin, of her substance: so that two whole and perfect Natures, that is to say, the Godhead and Manhood, were joined together in one Person, never to be divided."

- The Westminster Confession of Faith (1646), which contains the doctrinal statement of the entire Presbyterian world, says this: "The Son of God, the second person of the Trinity, being very and eternal God, of one substance and equal with the Father, did, when the fullness of time was come, take upon Him man's nature."

Throughout history, all branches of the Christian church have proclaimed that Jesus Christ is God, the eternal Creator of the universe.

WHAT DOES THE BIBLE SAY?

Since the Bible is our ultimate and final authority, what does God's Word say about Jesus Christ as God?

In Matthew 1:23 we read: " 'Behold, the virgin shall be with child, and bear a Son, and they shall call His name Immanuel,' which is translated, 'God with us.' " In His very naming, Jesus was "God with us"—God in human form.

In the first chapter of John's gospel we read: "In the beginning was the Word, and the Word was with God [the Father], and the Word *was God*.... All things were made through Him, and without Him nothing was made that was made.... And the Word became flesh and dwelt among us" (verses 1, 3, 14).

Jesus Himself said, "Most assuredly, I say to you, before Abraham was, I AM" (John 8:58).

After Jesus rose from the dead and showed His pierced hands and side to Thomas the doubter, Thomas fell at His feet and said, "My Lord and *my God*!" (John 20:28).

In Paul's letter to the Colossians, we read: "For it pleased the Father that in Him [Jesus] all the fullness should dwell" (1:19).

In Paul's letter to Titus, Jesus is called "our great God and Savior" (2:13).

The apostle John, in the closing words of his first epistle, describes Jesus as "the true God and eternal life" (5:20).

Even God the Father Himself addresses His Son in this way: "Your throne, *O God*, is forever and ever" (Hebrews 1:8, cited from Psalm 45:6).

So the Scriptures clearly teach that Jesus is God.

Many other evidences, perhaps less widely understood, are found in passages where the attributes of God the Father are also ascribed to Jesus Christ.

The Father is eternal. We're told that out of Bethlehem will come the One "whose goings forth are from of old, from everlasting" (Micah 5:2). The Babe from Bethlehem was eternally old when He was born.

The Father is omnipresent. Jesus said, "For where two or three are gathered together in My name, *I* am there in the midst of them" (Matthew 18:20). Not "I will be there" but "I am there." Every day of the week countless groups of believers meet in the name of Jesus Christ, and in every one of those groups, Jesus is there demonstrating His omnipresence—one of the attributes of deity.

The Father is immutable—unchangeable. This is one of the great attributes of deity. Scripture says, "Jesus Christ is the same yesterday, today, and forever" (Hebrews 13:8).

The Father is almighty. Creation demands omnipotence. Speaking about Jesus, the Bible says, "All things were made through Him, and without Him nothing was made that was made" (John 1:3). Jesus Christ is enthroned at God's right hand, "far above all principality and power and might and dominion" (Ephesians 1:21).

The Father comprehends all things. Peter said to Jesus, "Lord, You know all things" (John 21:17). And Jesus Himself said, "No one knows the Son except the Father. Nor does anyone know the Father except the Son" (Matthew 11:27). Commenting on this verse, the nineteenth-century British theologian Edward Bickersteth wrote, "He who knows the Father is omniscient; he who is known only by the Father is incomprehensible."[3]

The Father is the Creator, Preserver, and Governor of all things in heaven and earth. So also is Jesus Christ. Not only has He created all things, but He is "upholding all things by the word of His power" (Hebrews 1:3). "In him all things hold together" (Colossians 1:17, NIV).

The Father is the Searcher of hearts. So also is Christ, who says, "I am He who searches the minds and hearts" (Revelation 2:23).

The Father is the Most High Judge of all. Scripture says that all judgment is given into the hands of the Son: "For we must all appear before the judgment seat of Christ" (2 Corinthians 5:10).

So we see that all these attributes of deity are ascribed to Jesus Christ. But one attribute of deity is not ascribed to Jesus—the attribute of invisibility. For Jesus came to manifest the Father and make Him plainly visible. In Jesus Christ, we see the image of the eternal God.

More Evidence in Old Testament Prophecies

We find further evidence for the deity of Jesus in Old Testament prophecies that foretell the coming Christ.

In one of Isaiah's clear prophecies of the Messiah we read: "For unto us a Child is born, unto us a Son is given; and the government will be upon His shoulder. And His name will be called Wonderful, Counselor, *Mighty God, Everlasting Father,* Prince of Peace" (Isaiah 9:6).

There are other Old Testament prophecies that refer to Jehovah— "LORD"—and which are shown in the New Testament to be fulfilled by Jesus. For example, in Isaiah 40:3, we read, "The voice of one cry-ing in the wilderness: 'Prepare the way of the LORD [Jehovah]; make straight in the desert a highway for our God.'" John the Baptist attributed the same title to Jesus when he said in Matthew 3:3, "The voice of one [John the Baptist] crying in the wilderness: 'Prepare the way of the LORD [Jesus].'"

Another fascinating prophecy is found in Zechariah 12:10, where we read, "And I [Jehovah] will pour on the house…the Spirit of grace…then they will look on Me whom they pierced." In the New Testament we read, "And again another Scripture says, 'They shall look on Him [Christ] whom they pierced'" (John 19:37).

Who is Jehovah? Jehovah is the triune God. The Father is Jeho-vah; the Son is Jehovah; the Holy Spirit is Jehovah—the great "I AM."

Another evidence, often missed, is the fact that the Bible repeat-edly says we're to worship only God and no mere creature is ever to be worshiped. You'll recall in Revelation how John twice fell at the feet of the angel, but this heavenly messenger rebuked him and said he was not to worship an angel but to worship only God (Revelation 19:10; 22:8–9). To worship any creature is by definition blasphemy.

Yet again and again in Scripture we see Jesus Christ receiving worship from people and even blessing it. He was worshiped by the Magi, He was worshiped by those He healed, He was wor-shiped by the disciples, and He was worshiped by the women and the disciples after the resurrection. He was worshiped again and again. If Jesus were merely a creature, someone less than God, He would have been receiving and blessing the blasphemy of people.

When Thomas fell before Jesus and said, "My Lord and my God," and Jesus received his worship, He added these words:

Again and again in Scripture we see Jesus Christ receiving worship from people.

"Blessed are those who have not seen and yet have believed" (John 20:29).

JESUS CHRIST IS GOD

No mere man could hear the prayers of His people or answer them. This very day there are hundreds of millions of people lifting their hearts and voices in prayer to Jesus Christ in hundreds of languages. How does He understand all those prayers? If, indeed, He had taken a quick course in all the languages of the world and mastered each one, how does He hear them—millions at one time? He could not hear our prayers, much less answer them, if He were not God.

Alexander Whyte, the great pulpiteer of Scotland, said, "The longer I live, the firmer is my faith rooted in the Godhead of my Redeemer. No one short of the Son of God could meet my case. I must have one who is able to save to the utmost."[4]

Jesus Christ is God. Even Napoleon Bonaparte, who in his days of exile gave himself to studying the Scriptures, concluded, "I know men; and I tell you that Jesus Christ is no mere man. Between him and every other person in the world there is no possible term of comparison. Alexander, Caesar, Charlemagne, and I have founded empires. But on what did we rest the creations of our genius? Upon force. Jesus Christ founded his empire upon love; and at this hour millions of men would die for him."[5]

Earle Albert Rowell was a skeptic and an atheist who came to see the truth about Christ:

> I was reared an infidel. My parents and other immediate relatives were proud of their unbelief. I was nourished on the vaunting skeptics of the ages.

But I observed the futile amazement with which every skeptic from Celsus to Wells stood around the cradle of the Christ. I wondered why this helpless Babe was thrust into the world at a time when Roman greed, Jewish hate, and Greek subtlety would combine to crush Him. And yet this most powerful, devastating combination ever known in history served only to advance the cause of the Infant who was born in a stable....

No unbeliever could tell me why His words are as charged with power today as they were nineteen hundred years ago. Nor could scoffers explain how those pierced hands pulled human monsters with gnarled souls out of a hell of iniquity and overnight transformed them into steadfast, glorious heroes who died in torturing flames, that others might know the love and mighty power of the Christ who had given peace to their souls....

Nor could any scoffer explain, as Jesus Himself so daringly foretold, why...His words are piercing the densest forest, scaling the highest mountains, crossing the deepest seas and the widest deserts, making converts in every nation, kindred, tongue, and people on earth.

No doubter could tell me how this isolated Jew could utter words at once so simple that a child can understand them and so deep that the greatest thinkers cannot plumb their shining depths. The life, the words, the character of this strange Man are the enigma of history. Any naturalistic explanation makes Him a more puzzling paradox, a fathomless mystery.

But I learned that the paradox was plain and the mystery solved when I accepted Him for what He claimed to be—the

Son of God, come from heaven a Saviour of men, but above all, my own Saviour. I learned to thrill at the angel's words: "Behold…unto *you* is born this day…a Saviour, which is Christ the Lord." Now I have learned the great truth that

> "Though Christ a thousand times in Bethlehem be
> born,
> If He's not born in thee, thy soul is still forlorn."[6]

CONCLUSION

And so we see that once God became incarnate in Jesus Christ, it cannot be said He is hidden. He's no more hidden than the sun in the sky. The sun itself is a picture of the Son of God, for it is by Him that we see everything else.

Light from
an Empty Tomb

But Peter arose and ran to the tomb; and stooping down,
he saw the linen cloths lying by themselves;
and he departed,
marveling to himself at what had happened.

LUKE 24:12

Two billion people profess to believe that on the first Easter some two thousand years ago, Jesus of Nazareth, who was dead, arose and walked forth from the tomb. And each Easter, each year throughout the world, in every nation and from every kindred and tribe, groups have come from their homes and gathered to celebrate the resurrection of Christ from the dead.

This is the centerpiece of the Christian faith; this is the most important day all year. Why is it so important?

I was talking recently with an individual who said that for years she hadn't understood why the fact that Jesus rose from the dead so long ago was of such importance to us.

Why is it important?

First of all, because it's the "Gibraltar" of Christianity. It's the massive rock foundation upon which the entire superstructure of the

Christian faith rests. Destroy that foundation, and the entire fabric of Christianity crumbles.

This has been well understood by all the skeptics, from Pontius Pilate to today's James Cameron, producer of *Titanic* and more recently an antiresurrection movie. Therefore, all their largest critical guns have been aimed at the resurrection of Christ.

But Christ's resurrection still stands—like a mighty anvil surrounded by hundreds of broken hammers, undaunted by all the assaults of unbelief. The eminence of the resurrection of Christ lifts it above all the other doctrines of mankind.

Second, the resurrection of Christ is important because it answers the most crucial question people can ever ask, a question that has haunted the minds of humans from time immemorial. Early in the Bible, Job asks, "If a man dies, shall he live again?" (14:14). I venture to say there's not one person who hasn't at some time asked, "When I die, will I live again?" All other problems are simply pale shadows of that dark enigma. All other problems we face are simply adumbrations, or foreshadowings, of that problem. War leads to death. Poverty leads to death. Sickness leads to death. Aging leads to death. Failure can lead to death. Only in Jesus Christ is death conquered.

> Only Christ has conquered death.

He was the divine God-man. This is made apparent according to a principle He Himself enunciated: "He who is greatest among you shall be your servant" (Matthew 23:11). The one who therefore renders the greatest service to mankind is the greatest among us. And no one has rendered any service comparable to that of Christ, who burst the bonds of death and overcame the terror of the grave, removing the sting from that awful, final foe of man. Only Christ has conquered death. Jesus has no peer.

I continue to be astonished at the vast multitudes of people who go blithely through life asserting, most emphatically, that the idea of Jesus's rising from the dead is nonsense. They say, "Of course He couldn't have risen from the dead. People don't rise from the dead. It's not even worth our contemplation. People who believe it simply do so on the basis of blind, unreasoning, ignorant faith."

Is that true? Satan is still the chief of liars, the father of lies, and what he tells is exactly the opposite of the truth. It's true that all other religions are based on blind faith—a fact we won't deny. They're based simply on the authoritative assertion of those who would propagate their religion. You're to believe it, you pay your nickel, and you take your choice.

THE EVIDENCE FOR THE RESURRECTION

But Christianity is different. It is unique. It's the only religion (other than its root, Judaism) based upon historical evidence—the only historic, evidential religion in the world. And that's a fact of surpassing importance. Let's consider a few of the people who are most qualified to pass judgment on such matters as these. Come with me across the ocean to England, to a land renowned for its jurisprudence. To whom shall we speak who is authoritative on this subject?

Let's talk to the Lord Chief Justice of England, Lord Darling, who held that position some years ago. He at one time attended a dinner party where the conversation turned to the subject of religion and, more particularly, to a book that attacked the resurrection of Christ. Finally the people present turned to Lord Darling and asked his opinion on the matter. He sat back in his chair, put his fingers together in the way he often used to do when meditating behind the bench as the Lord Chief Justice, and gave his answer.

Lord Darling said that Christians are asked to take a lot on faith, such as the teachings of Jesus or the miracles of Jesus. He added that if we had to take *all* on faith, he for one would be skeptical. The crux of the problem of whether Jesus was who He claimed to be must surely depend, Lord Darling explained, upon the truth or falsehood of the Resurrection. And on that most important point, he added, we aren't merely asked to have faith. He said that in its favor, as a living truth, there existed such overwhelming evidence—positive, factual, and circumstantial evidence—so that no intelligent jury in the world could fail to bring in a verdict that the resurrection of Christ was true.

> *No intelligent jury in the world could fail to bring in a verdict that the resurrection of Christ was true.*

Or if you prefer homegrown authorities on this subject, may I direct your attention to Simon Greenleaf, a professor at Harvard Law School in the nineteenth century who was cited by the chief justice of the United States as the greatest authority in the history of the world on legal evidences. He wrote vast tomes on the laws of evidences. Some of the students in his classes challenged him to apply the laws of evidence to the historicity of the resurrection of Jesus. Being the world's foremost authority on the subject of evidence, he agreed to do just that. He took each strand of the evidence for the resurrection of Christ and laid it out, one strand after another, after another, after another. He then applied the scorching acids of criticism and investigation. He turned the brightest lights of critical examination by the laws of evidence on each thread of evidence.

When he finished, he wrote a book entitled *The Testimony of the Evangelists,* a study in the application of the basic rules of common law to the witness borne by the evangelists Matthew, Mark, Luke, and John. In that book he concluded that if the evidence for the resurrection of Jesus Christ were set forth before any unbiased jury in the world, they would inevitably conclude that the resurrection of Christ is historic fact.

You don't have to be a world-renowned authority like Simon Greenleaf to learn the truth of Christ's resurrection. Just take the trouble to look and see—something that, tragically, many people don't bother to do.

In addition to blind faith, there's also something called blind unbelief. It's unbelief without examining the evidence. Millions of people walk and live and die in blind unbelief. As the hymn writer put it:

> Blind unbelief is sure to err, and scan His work in vain.
> God is His own interpreter, and He will make it
>   plain.[1]

In the years after the Civil War, two friends who were both former officers were on a train together. One of them, who had served as a Union general during the war, was a skeptic who couldn't bring himself to believe in the resurrection of Christ. His views were no doubt influenced by the strong agnosticism of his well-known friend, Robert G. Ingersoll, who was a traveling lecturer winning renown for his anti-Christian oratory.

As they rode the train together, the men's conversation turned to religion, and Ingersoll suggested to the general that since he had talent as a writer, he should write a book destroying the myth of Jesus as the God-man who had risen from the dead. He told the general to present Jesus as He really was, simply a man among men, someone who lived and died and that was the end of it.

The general decided to do just that.

Carefully he conducted historical research and gathered evidence, then examined and studied all the pertinent facts. Finally, after a number of years, the book was completed and published.

It was an immediate success, selling millions of copies, and it's still in print today. You may have read it or seen the movie version, entitled *Ben-Hur: A Tale of the Christ.* The man who wrote the book was General Lew Wallace. He had taken up the task his friend suggested but was converted to Christ in the midst of it. His book, instead of showing Jesus to be a mere man, presents Him as the divine Savior from heaven, who lived and died a sacrificial death for our sins and rose from the dead as conqueror over the grave. All this because General Lew Wallace bothered to collect and examine the evidence.

A Summary of the Evidence

When we talk about the *evidence* for the Resurrection that convinced these scholars who studied it, what are we referring to?

Here is the claim: Jesus rose from the dead—bodily—and appeared to over five hundred eyewitnesses in the following forty days, offering many convincing proofs. This is what is reported in the New Testament (1 Corinthians 15:3–6; Acts 1:3).

Dr. Edwin Yamauchi, professor of Ancient History at Miami University, Ohio, is a New Testament scholar. He notes: "Christianity, of course, is based on the belief in the resurrection of Jesus. Now, how can you explain the expansion of this religion that exalted a man who suffered the ignominious death, the worst possible death reserved for criminals and slaves, crucifixion? How can you explain the growth and the expansion of this religion without the Resurrection? You cannot. Now, some scholars have tried to do that, but they do not offer any convincing explanation."[2]

Dr. D. A. Carson, professor at Trinity Evangelical Divinity School, is also a scholar. He observes, "There is no parallel in the ancient world, for example, that has the disclosure of a person risen from the dead to 500 people. There is just nothing like that in the ancient world."[3] Josh McDowell, author of *Evidence That Demands a Verdict*, fleshes out the implications of the risen Jesus being seen by so many people: "Well, you take 500 people who personally saw Jesus as an eyewitness after the Resurrection, give each one of them six minutes in a court of law to testify, you would have 3,000 minutes of eyewitness testimony; that's 50 hours...when in many criminal cases, you only need one eyewitness to convict a person."[4]

Another line of reasoning involves the empty tomb. Dr. Paul L. Maier, professor of Ancient History at Western Michigan University, is a best-selling author and Harvard-trained historian. He points out, "We often overlook the empty tomb, but I think the empty tomb is very important, because that is something an ancient historian can get at.... Where did Christianity first begin in terms of the organized proclamation that Jesus rose from the dead? Only one place on earth: Jerusalem. There, least of all, could Christianity ever have gotten started if the moldering body of Jesus of Nazareth were available anytime after Sunday morning."[5]

Ultimately, the incredible change of the disciples after Jesus appeared to them is what convinces us about the historicity of Jesus's resurrection. N. T. Wright, Bishop of Durham in England, says, "The disciples, at the time of Jesus' crucifixion, were completely devastated. Everybody in their world knew that if you were following a prophet or a Messiah or a leader or whatever and that person got executed by the Roman authorities, it meant you had backed the wrong horse. Since everybody knew that a crucified Messiah was a failed Messiah, the only thing that explains why they said Jesus was the

Messiah is that they really did believe He had been bodily raised from the dead…. What we're looking at with the Resurrection is the birth of God's new world, of a whole new mode of being. That is why I think the disciples found it so incredibly difficult to get their minds turned around right from the beginning. They were absolutely clear that the tomb was empty, that they had seen Jesus, and that this really was that which the prophets had spoken about, even though they weren't expecting it. So, I believe it, because, as a Christian, all my life I have found that it makes sense of everything else. But, as a historian, I find that all the lines point in towards saying, 'This is far and away the best explanation for why early Christianity began and why it told the stories it did.' "[6]

In short, He is risen. He is risen indeed!

THE SIGNIFICANCE OF THE RESURRECTION

Next we must consider the *significance* of the Resurrection. What does it mean? Is it some strange phenomenon that happened millenniums ago and has little to do with us today?

Not at all. It is of transforming import to our lives.

Jesus said, "Because I live, you will live also" (John 14:19). The light that streams forth from His empty tomb lightens our own lives and futures. In the light of Christ's promise, millions of Christians have lived and ended their lives rejoicing. The resurrection of Christ is a promise of our resurrection—Christ as the firstfruits, and we as the full harvest.

The Bible also says that God raised Him up for our justification. What does that mean?

It means first that if Christ had merely died on the cross and been buried in a tomb—His body covered, forgotten, and rotting in the grave—how would we know if Jesus had truly been a sacrifice for sin and that this sacrifice was accepted by God? How could we ever know?

We couldn't. But because God raised Him from the dead, God has declared unto the world that He has accepted the sacrifice His Son made and that those who trust in Him are justified from all the things they couldn't have been justified from under the law.

This means that in the resurrection of Christ, there's forgiveness for our sins and justification for those who will trust in Him.

The Resurrection proves the deity of Jesus. Therefore, God is anything but hidden. He Himself has joined His own creation, once and for all.

The further significance of Christ's resurrection is that it brings victory in our lives right now. Christ conquers all the problems of humanity; He gives meaning to our lives.

The Resurrection proves the deity of Jesus.

Can you imagine how meaningless life really is to those who are without Christ, without God, and without hope in this world? I'm reminded of the ephemerid, a small flylike insect sometimes called the mayfly or the dayfly. It's a peculiar little insect with four wings, but it lacks something most of us like to have—a mouth. Having no mouth, it doesn't eat, and in not eating, it lives for only a few hours or a few days at most. Therefore it gets its name from the word *ephemeral,* which means "passing away." How insignificant their lives must be. What difference does it make what they do? Who knows? Who cares? They come and they go, and they're forgotten.

On a cosmic scale, is it not the same with people? If we're simply creatures of this life and this world comes and goes, the day will come when this whole solar system will have fallen into the dark hole of entropy, and the second law of thermodynamics will have brought everything to a heat death. The world as we know it will be no more.

There'll be no significance to our lives; there will have been no significance. *Sign*ificance points to a *sign,* and the sign must be seen. But there'll be no one to see it or even read the history. Therefore, our lives will have been nothing but sound and fury, signifying nothing.

No, only Jesus Christ, who opens a portal on eternity, gives meaning and significance to our lives.

Many have thought their future was finished. But if you're in Jesus Christ, your future hasn't even begun. Jesus will make us even more new than we were the day before. What an incredible thought. Because He conquered death, one day He will still the wheel of time, and time shall be no more. All loneliness and unhappiness will be done away with, and we shall be brought into that paradise He has gone to prepare.

Many are worried about this problem-filled world in which we live. We see nations that appear to be on collision courses. It seems inevitable that this world will go up in one great nuclear holocaust. One day the button will be pushed, and there'll be a great exchange of missiles flying over the whole world. There'll be nothing then but the withering wastes of the once-verdant land.

But Jesus Christ has come forth from the grave and is riding on His white horse, going forth conquering and to conquer. All the rulers of this world rule only according to His command. He raises up nations and casts them down. His will does inexorably come to pass. His kingdom will come, because Christ is the sovereign Lord of this world.

In that we can rejoice. And how great it is.

The Experience of the Resurrection

We must also consider the fact of the *experience* of the Resurrection, because, yes, you can experience the Resurrection in your own life.

It's not until Jesus Christ comes into our lives—until He throws aside that stony wall encasing our hearts, until He bursts the bonds of death and darkness and brings heaven's light into our souls—that we can *know* for sure Christ is risen, because *we* have risen with Him.

How can we rise with Christ? By identifying with Him. Where must we begin?

I would take you to the *Scala Sancta,* the reputed sacred stairs that once were before Pilate's palace and upon which Jesus stood when the accusations were piled upon Him, one after another, and Jesus opened not His mouth. Why? Because He was guilty. He was silent because He was guilty with your guilt and mine. He was bearing upon Himself our sins and taking unto His own body our punishment.

Identify with Him as the sentence is passed. He is declared to be worthy of death, and He's given into the hands of those who would crucify Him. The sentence of condemnation is given.

We stand condemned with Jesus Christ, and we're led off to be crucified with Him. Identify with Him. Know that He is going in *your* place, that He's hanging upon that cross on *your* behalf. It's for *you* that He's suffering this cruel death and terrible passion. Identify with the One who is dying for you—with His death and with His burial—and then you can identify with Him in His resurrection, being raised in newness of life, quickened by the Spirit of God, made alive in Jesus Christ. By faith you can identify with the One who is your substitute in death and in resurrection and whom you can join in both.

> We stand condemned with Jesus Christ.

FACING DEATH

I was once asked to conduct the funeral of a man I'd been acquainted with off and on. He wasn't known to be a Christian, but

I didn't know him well enough to really say. The service was held in a funeral parlor where they had the usual arrangements. Looking at the casket, I could see just the top of his face and a slight bit of his body. Before I stood to speak, someone came and slowly closed the lid of the casket, and I watched as it lowered over him. Then they locked it. I remember thinking, *And now, my friend, who's going to get you out of there?*

There's no one who empties a tomb like Jesus—a tomb or a casket. Scratch that, because that's not really accurate. There's no one who empties a tomb or a casket *besides* Jesus—no one else at all.

Donald Grey Barnhouse was the name of my spiritual father. He was a brilliant minister in Philadelphia with a nationwide radio program. He was a linguist, a scholar, and a powerful preacher. He once told of an encounter he'd had with a man who was a virulent atheist, a man who had no use for Christianity and described the whole thing as poppycock. He said he didn't need Christ or any religious stuff.

They parted. Time went by—two years, in fact—and Barnhouse heard that this man was in the hospital, at the edge of the valley of the shadow of death. So Barnhouse went to the hospital, found the man's room, slipped quietly in, and took a seat in the corner. He folded his hands and sat and did nothing else. When the man finally saw him, he said, "What are you doing here?"

He responded, "Oh, nothing. You told me you were an atheist and that you weren't afraid to die, and I've always wanted to watch an atheist die, so I just came over to watch. I'm not going to do anything. You go ahead with whatever it is you're doing, and I'll just watch."

A look of unutterable grief and horror came over the man's face, and he said, "You wouldn't mock a dying man, would you?" Then he asked Dr. Barnhouse to tell him again about Christ and about the

Cross and about the Resurrection. Before the hour was out, the sun of righteousness had risen in the valley of the shadow.

No Longer a Terror

A Christian need have no fear of death. I'm not afraid of death, for this extraordinary and remarkable reason: I'm never going to die. Jesus said it clearly Himself: "Whoever lives and believes in Me *shall never die*" (John 11:26). He didn't say He would make death more comfortable for those who believe or more pleasant or more optimistic. He said we would never die.

Oh yes, this mortal flesh dies—but *we* will never die. That dark, cold river we're supposed to cross doesn't exist for us. Christ has transformed that symbol of death; it is now the portal into paradise.

> *This mortal flesh dies— but we will never die.*

This has been attested to by countless people who have experienced what we call death and who have come back to say, "I never died. People were looking at my body, and I was watching them watch, but I was alive. I hadn't died." Thus the Prince of life offers us the only eraser that can eradicate that appointment.

The day of death is not on my calendar, and it doesn't need to be on yours. You do not have to die. You can simply step into the presence of the glorified One. You can enter into paradise, where there's no more pain or suffering or sorrow or tears. You can join that vast multitude of people made perfect by Christ to dwell in the city of light, where fountains sparkle forever and flowers are ever blooming. You can smile with the smile of the twinkling stars as you're plumed with the plume of never-ending life.

How glorious it is that we shall be with Him who has overcome death through His cross and resurrection.

Life-After-Death Experiences

Paul, the great apostle to the Gentiles, was preaching the gospel in a certain city when his opponents stirred up a riot. In the scene described in Acts 14:19–20, Paul was stoned, then dragged outside the walls of the city, where he was left for dead. Sometime later, he arose and went back into the city.

That's the historical occasion, according to most biblical scholars, for this experience recorded by the apostle:

> I know a man in Christ who fourteen years ago—whether in
> the body I do not know, or whether out of the body I do not
> know, God knows—such a one was caught up to the third
> heaven. And I know such a man—whether in the body or out
> of the body I do not know, God knows—how he was caught
> up into Paradise and heard inexpressible words, which it is
> not lawful for a man to utter. (2 Corinthians 12:2–4)

This was one of the first recorded experiences of someone apparently dying and having a glimpse of the world to come.

Over the years there have been other such occasions, but they've been sporadic. However, in recent decades with modern resuscitation methods, these cases are multiplying extraordinarily. Now more than 50 percent of people who suddenly drop dead can be resuscitated, unless there are massive bodily injuries.

This has given rise to all sorts of questions and speculations. Many are familiar with the writings of Dr. Elisabeth Kübler-Ross and Dr. Raymond Moody, psychiatrists who have investigated the stories of hundreds of people who have reported these experiences after coming face to face with what could be called clinical death.

There has been a great storm of controversy surrounding their stories, as one might expect. Meanwhile, the data continues to come forth.

All sorts of cases have been reported where people supposedly died, then they claimed to see a white light or something similar. Most of the people who experienced this after-death experience seemed to report pleasant sensations. This had led some people to believe that perhaps everybody ends up going to heaven.

Dr. Maurice Rawlings has written a book on this, titled *To Hell and Back*. He's an expert in the diagnosis of cardiovascular disease. He also was a complete skeptic concerning life after death. But his whole view about life and death changed because of an encounter with a patient, a forty-eight-year-old man who was a rural mail carrier. The man complained of pains in his chest. They put him on a treadmill and connected up the EKG to see if it really was a heart problem. The man slowly began to walk and then jog.

The man was screaming, "I'm in hell!"

Instead of the EKG registering abnormalities and his heart fibrillating, his heart suddenly just stopped. The man dropped dead on the office floor. There was no other doctor in the building at the time, so Dr. Rawlings began to perform emergency resuscitation methods, massaging his heart and giving him artificial respiration. After a while the man came to, and he was screaming, "I'm in hell!" This happened intermittently, with the man dying and resuscitating and yelling, "I'm in hell!"

Dr. Rawlings saw that the man's eyes were completely dilated, perspiration covered his face, he had an expression of sheer horror, and his hair was standing on end. With pleas and groanings, he urged the doctor not to let him go back to hell again. A wave of panic hit the doctor like nothing he'd ever experienced. He realized that this man, whenever his heart stopped, was indeed experiencing something beyond extinction.

Eventually the man was fully resuscitated. Two days later Dr. Rawlings went to the man's hospital room with a pencil and paper. He was curious. He wanted to question the man about his experiences and record them. If there was a hell, he wanted to find out what it looked like.

But to the doctor's utter astonishment, when he asked the man about his experiences, he responded, "What hell?" Suddenly the doctor realized that this experience had been so traumatic, so painful to the man's psyche, that the human mind had done what it often does under such circumstances: it had repressed the memory, and it was gone.

From this and similar cases he investigated, Dr. Rawlings discovered why so many of the reported experiences indicated people having pleasant experiences. He noted that Dr. Kübler-Ross and Dr. Moody were psychiatrists and, to his knowledge, had never resuscitated anyone. Unless you get the account immediately on the spot, before the human mind has a chance to repress it and suppress it, it will be lost forever.

Dr. Rawlings has been researching this for some years now, and he has found that of the people who've been resuscitated, at least as many report terrifying, horrible experiences as report good ones.

CONCLUSION

The only way to eternal life is the Cross of Jesus Christ. The only way to heaven is through trusting in Him and resting in Him who died and went to hell and experienced it in our place. God has revealed the eternal outcome of our lives, and He has done all that's necessary for eternal life.

Coauthor Jerry Newcombe notes that Dr. Kennedy himself experienced the very heaven he had been pointing others to for such a long time, when he died on September 5, 2007. During his funeral, which was packed and televised, a portion of the audio from a sermon he had preached just a few years before was played. This is what the congregants heard that day (in a service that honored his express wishes contained in this paragraph):

> Now, I know that someday I am going to come to what some people will say is the end of this life. They will probably put me in a box and roll me right down here in front of the church, and some people will gather around, and a few people will cry. But I have told them not to do that because I don't want them to cry. I want them to begin the service with the Doxology and end with the "Hallelujah" chorus, because I am not going to be there, and I am not going to be dead. I will be more alive than I have ever been in my life, and I will be looking down upon you poor people who are still in the land of dying and have not yet joined me in the land of the living. And I will be alive forevermore, in greater health and vitality and joy than ever, ever, I or anyone has known before.

PART III

FINDING
HIM

How to Know God

God is faithful, by whom you were called
into the fellowship of His Son, Jesus Christ our Lord.
1 CORINTHIANS 1:9

The story is told of a pleasant dinner gathering with about twenty guests, among whom were an actor and a minister. Someone asked the actor if he would do a dramatic reading of the Twenty-third Psalm. He began, "The Lord is my shepherd…" and recited the full psalm from memory with great beauty and style. Everyone was impressed and applauded him greatly.

After a pause, someone asked the minister to recite the same passage. He was reluctant to follow such an act, but they prevailed upon him. He too had memorized the sacred words, and he too delivered them verbatim. After he finished, there was a hush, followed by tepid applause.

But the actor was impressed. He stood up and declared, "I may know the psalm." Then he pointed to the minister and said, "But our guest here knows the Shepherd."

It's one thing to know *about* God. It's quite another to *know* God. Up to this point, we've talked about faith in God, evidence for God, and the fact that God is revealed in Christ. Now we want to talk about knowing Him personally. When we know Him, even if some dark shadows may come our way and obscure Him, we have the quiet assurance that He is indeed there and not hidden after all.

LOOKING FOR LOOPHOLES

One of the great comedians of the twentieth century was W. C. Fields, who in his professional persona seemed to be in a continual state of inebriation—the kind of man whose view of the world was totally cockeyed, the kind of guy who could say, "Well, anyone who hates dogs and children couldn't be all bad." He also held religion in disdain, along with godly morals.

When he came to the final illness of his life, he was in the hospital, and doctors gave him little hope of surviving. One day a friend who had known him well for many years walked into the hospital room. To his shock, there before his eyes was W. C. Fields reading the Bible in his hospital bed.

Many people are looking for loopholes.

The friend asked in utter amazement, "What in the world are you doing?"

W. C. Fields replied (with his inimitable accent), "Just looking for loopholes...looking for loopholes."

It seems to me there are many people who are looking for loopholes, who are trying to find some way to escape the just consequences of their sins. I suppose they've tried every conceivable way, from denying there's a God who could possibly punish them, to denying there's a hell where they could be punished or denying that a loving God would ever send anyone there—even such reprobates as themselves. They've been doing what people constantly do: trying to justify themselves by condemning God. By proving that God is unjust and unfair and unloving, they conclude that they themselves must be, by comparison, pretty decent folks.

But is it true? Does God *have* to give everyone a chance to be saved? Must God extend mercy to all?

Many people say, "Yes, God must extend mercy to every sinner," and yet by their own actions, they prove their inconsistency on this.

Question: Did you ever give money to a beggar?

Second question: Have you given money to *every* beggar you've seen in your entire life?

I would guess that you haven't. But suppose I were to respond, "How dare you! What do you mean by refusing to give money to every single beggar you encounter? Who do you think you are? Why, you act as if it's *your* money!"

You might answer, "Well, it is. I worked for it. I earned it. It's mine. And who is this beggar, anyway? I never saw him before. He never did anything for me. He doesn't work for me. Why should I give any beggar money? I'm not required to do so."

All that, of course, is true.

To change the metaphor, suppose the president of the United States decides to pardon a criminal in prison. Do you think people in America would rise up in righteous indignation and *demand* that he open the doors of every prison in the country and turn loose a couple of million criminals on the populace of America? Of course not.

When Christ was skewered to that cross, lifted up naked for all the world to see, He was bearing the shame and the horror and the agony and the pain of the worst kind of human suffering that could be endured. For three interminable hours He hung there, until at last there came high noon.

At the peak of that day's heat, suddenly the sun's light failed, and a great darkness descended, a blackness that covered the earth. There in that darkness, unseen by mortal eyes, a hand came down from heaven and extended before Jesus's face that cup containing the sin of the world, and it was placed to His lips. Willingly Jesus drank it down to the very dregs, and the Scriptures tell us that Jesus Christ, the Holy One of God, became sin for us: "For He [God the Father] made Him who knew no sin to be sin for us, that we might become the righteousness of God in Him" (2 Corinthians 5:21). God the Father, who loved His Son with an infinite and eternal love, dumped over the cauldron of His wrath for sin, and that wrath fell upon His own Son. At last, when it seemed an eternity had passed, Jesus cried, "It is finished! It is done! *Tetelestai*—the debt is paid in full." (See John 19:30.)

Though I don't know if W. C. Fields found it, there *is* a loophole. Jesus created it with His own agony and anguish upon the cross. There's a portal that leads to paradise—only one, and all who enter therein through the Cross shall receive eternal life.

THE ONLY MEDIATOR

There are degrees of punishment, and as Jesus said, "For everyone to whom much is given, from him much will be required; and to whom much has been committed, of him they will ask the more" (Luke 12:48).

Therefore, those who sit in church and hear the gospel of grace and the love of Jesus Christ, yet never open their hearts and surrender their lives to Him, will receive an infinitely greater punishment than a headhunter in Africa who has sinned against nothing but the candlelight of creation and conscience. But they're all without excuse and all in need of that one Mediator between God and mankind—Christ Jesus.

This Mediator exercises a threefold office—of Prophet, Priest, and King. Jesus is all three simultaneously. As Prophet, He saves us from our ignorance of sin; as Priest, He saves us from the guilt of sin; as King, He saves us from the dominion of sin over our lives.

We might understand these offices of Christ better when we note their similarity to something in our lives. Adam was a prophet from God to speak for God and to God. He was also a priest, not in any executory sense to pay for sin (because at that point there was none), but as one who was to love God and to consecrate himself to His service. He was also a king who was to have dominion over the earth and to subdue it, order it, and reign over it in the name of God above. So Adam was prophet, priest, and king—unto God, and under God.

Each fallen person is now a false prophet.

But then Adam sinned and by his disobedience fell. Through his fall, our nature was corrupted, and we came under the influence of evil. We were subjected to the powers of Satan, but still we maintain this threefold office. Each fallen person is now a prophet, but a false prophet—a prophet of Satan—and so he spews out lies, false philosophy, and false science, maintaining that humanity has risen from the slime and not from God. False religions, heresies, cults, and "isms" of all sorts have come along to distort and pervert the teachings of Scripture. All manner of radical denials are abroad in the church today—denials of Scripture, denials of the deity of Christ and His miracles, denials of His virgin birth, and denials of His resurrection. A false prophet is what fallen humanity has become under the dominion of Satan, continually spewing forth the devil's lies, corrupting generation after generation. Jesus said that by the traditions of our fathers, we've become corrupt and have made void the law of God. This is the nature of fallen humanity.

This historical situation in the fall of man began with Adam, continues down through the centuries, and will finally culminate in the Antichrist, who again bears the threefold mediatorial office. He's the false prophet incarnate who comes to bring the culmination of all the lies against Christ and against God. The book of Revelation reveals the false prophets who ultimately shall be cast into the lake of fire.

The Antichrist is also the false priest in the culmination of all false priests who have led countless millions astray through their false teachings of salvation by human merit.

Finally, as the false king, having usurped or attempted to usurp dominion over the world, the Antichrist reveals himself as that one who would trample underfoot, by the power of his kingdom, those who oppose him.

But against this culminating threefold power of evil, we find that Christ has come as the Mediator sent from God—the true Prophet, the true Priest, the true King.

Certainly in His incarnate life, He was that perfect Prophet. Jesus spoke the things that He heard from His Father. His teaching was perfect, and people have never ceased to marvel at what He said.

VOLUNTARY VERSUS INVOLUNTARY LOVE

During World War II, the custom here in the United States was to put a lonely gold star in the window when parents lost a son in the war effort. That was very poignant and very tragic. We all understand what that meant to families.

However, if we looked at it carefully, we would see that in some cases, perhaps even most, the parents did not *give* their sons. In many instances their sons were ripped out of their grasp by the draft. Many parents did everything they could to keep their sons out of the military. God, on the other hand, freely and voluntarily gave up His Son for us. He gave Him up in order that God may be God.

God gave His only Son—His *only Son.* When we have a child, that child is in our image and lives in our home. Over the years the bond with our child develops and deepens. (If you have a daughter who happens to be almost perfect, like mine, and you've had her in your home for decades, you certainly know the strength of this bond.) Jesus Christ is the express image of the Father, and He has been with Him forever, not just for a few years or a couple of decades. So imagine what kind of a bond was thus torn in two when the Father gave His Son to die for the world.

So rich is the love of God for us, love that is best seen in His Son suffering on the cross in our place.

SIN WILL BE PUNISHED

One day everyone reading this book and every person in this world will bow their knees before Christ and acknowledge that He's the sovereign Lord of all. For some, this will be a time of great, climactic joy as we do in person what we've done a thousand times before. For others, it will be their last act before they're taken and dropped into hell.

It all depends on whether your kneeling before Christ was done in this world, while the day of grace was still shining upon you and while the free offer of eternal life was still open. Jesus tells us to come unto Him, and He will give us eternal life.

Have you come to Him? Have you bowed the knee and received that free forgiveness, that free pardon, that ticket to opening night in paradise? If you don't have that, you won't be there. Receive Him now as your Savior…rather than face Him later as your Judge. Our sin will be paid for, either by Christ on the cross or by us in hell. It's one or the other.

If you've never accepted Jesus Christ as your Savior and Lord, I ask you to pray this or a similar prayer:

> O Lord Jesus, I bow my heart and head and knee before You. You are the King eternal, invincible. You are the sovereign Lord of all. I surrender myself to You right now. I place my trust and hope of eternal life in what You've done for me on the cross. I abandon all delusions that I am good, for You have declared that there are none good, that all have sinned and come short of Your glory. And so I accept You as my righteousness. Clothe me with Your perfect obedience that I may stand faultless before Your throne. All this, with joy, I pray. In Your name, O Christ. Amen.

If you prayed that prayer sincerely, you've begun the greatest adventure that you could ever take. And I strongly urge you to begin to read the Bible and to pray every day. If you've never read the Bible before, start with the gospel of John (the fourth book of the New Testament). I also urge you to get involved with a Bible-based, Bible-believing church.

If you would like a free book to help you become established in the Christian faith, write to Coral Ridge Ministries and ask for *Beginning Again.*[1]

Once we know Jesus as our personal Lord and Savior, our thank-you to Him for His gift of salvation will be to serve Him in every area of our lives. Good works will flow naturally from our lives, as good apples grow naturally on a good apple tree.

CONCLUSION

When we know God personally, when we enjoy fellowship with Him personally, then He's anything but hidden. We know God in our hearts because He first reached out to us.

10

Wise Men
Seek Him Still

Where is He who has been born King of the Jews?
For we have seen His star in the East
and have come to worship Him.

MATTHEW 2:2

G od is no longer hidden since He has revealed Himself through His Son. But not everybody seeks Him, of course. Many insist on walking in darkness, lest their evil deeds be exposed. But there are wise people, even today, who still seek Him.

THE MAGI

Come with me on a trip across thousands of miles and thousands of years to that great expanse of Arabian Desert lying east of Jerusalem.

On this portentous night, you'll note the air is crisp and chill. The black canvas of the sky coruscates with a thousand sparkling diamonds. But beneath, the world is still. The desert winds, which throughout the day have piled high the shifting sands, have ceased their play, and now all is at rest. Silence hangs ominously over the earth—a silence that seems to press down upon the soul, silence as of a tomb awaiting the bright sound of the resurrection morn.

If you peer deeply into the darkness, you can see in the distance, to the east, even darker shadows approaching. As you look closely, you can at last make out the silhouettes of the desert camels approaching on padded feet, silently making their way to Bethlehem. It's the visit of the wise men from the East, that beautiful, almost ethereal story that has enshrined itself in the hearts of mankind as a part of Christmastime. The visit of the Magi. The wise men of the East who have traveled far, who have come to worship the Babe at Bethlehem. The wise men who were the harbingers of a vast host of other Gentiles who would come to Christ to worship Him.

The wise men *sought* Him, we're told, and wise men seek Him still.

The Magi probably were not kings. The word *magoi* is Greek, from which we get the word *magician.* Perhaps they were astrologers or philosophers. They were likely from Persia (Iran) or Babylonia (Iraq) and had come a great distance to worship Christ, having received some portent of His birth in that strange and singular occurrence in the sky.

> Truly wise men will ever seek after Jesus Christ.

I wonder what they would say to us if they could be here today. Why would these men, renowned through the centuries for their wisdom, inconvenience themselves to travel so far to see a baby?

I think their answer to such a question would be the very epitome of wisdom—that truly wise men will ever seek after Jesus Christ.

WHAT ARE PEOPLE SEEKING?

I'm afraid few people today are seeking after truth. Truth hasn't been the popular quest of our time. Ours is a day when people seek after other things, such as pleasure. Ours is, no doubt, a day of hedonism.

Someone said to me recently that when he was in college he discovered the word *hedonist,* and he thought excitedly, *Why, that's what I am.* He told all his friends he was a hedonist, "one who lives for pleasure." We live in a culture saturated with hedonism. It's all around us. It constantly batters our senses. It's a sensate culture, a culture that tells us, "Enjoy yourself. This life is all there is."

No doubt millions have sung that song and have never questioned the philosophy behind it. But that philosophy is totally antithetical to what's taught in the Bible. The Bible declares that our lives are but vapors that rise up and pass away. They're like the grass that grows in the morning and in the evening is cut down. Our lives, indeed, are fleeting.

However, the admonition of Scripture is not simply to spend our short lives enjoying ourselves. It's not to grab all the gusto we can. Scripture doesn't say, "Well, life is to enjoy, is it not?" But in our hedonistic culture, doesn't everyone hold to that philosophy? It isn't even questioned. It isn't open to debate. It's a conclusion that the vast majority of the masses of this country and the world have reached.

Jesus said, "I must work the works of Him who sent Me while it is day; the night is coming when no one can work" (John 9:4). Serve the Lord now, for the moment is coming when this life will all be past and there'll be no further opportunity to serve Christ on earth.

The truth as to what our lives are all about is to be found in Jesus Christ. He tells us the truth about the questions that have plagued the minds of people down through the centuries—the questions college students bat around in dormitories: Who am I? Where did I come from? Where am I going? Why am I here? The answers to those questions can be found only in Jesus Christ.

Where did you come from? A great many people would say, "You came from slime. You wiggled and squirmed and crawled and scratched and swung by your tail until…here you are. Scratch the surface of mankind a little bit, and you'll find the tiger or the ape." This philosophy has been the greatest contribution to the brutalization of mankind we've ever known. What was the result of Hitler espousing such teaching? He treated people like rats—carved on them, experimented on them, and killed them by the millions, in the same way we might exterminate roaches. Why have the proponents of communism killed countless millions, some say more than a hundred million people? Because communists consider people to be simply complicated animals, and they deal with them as they would a monkey.

On the other hand, if we aren't creatures of the slime but have been created by the Creator, we've been made for a heavenly inheritance. If we've been made in the image of God and not in the image of a lizard, that's an entirely different picture. If I'm the son of the eternal God, then my life has a transcendent meaning. Where I come from tells a great deal about who I am.

That's one reason so many people today are eagerly searching for their roots. They want to find out where they came from in order that they might answer the question *Who am I?* But we need to go back further than simply five or ten generations. We need to go back to the beginning and find out whether we came out of the slime and the mud or from the hand of the omniscient God. The resultant attitude in our hearts about who we are will determine how we approach life, and that attitude may easily determine the future of the human race.

Why are we here? Those wise men would tell us that only in Jesus Christ can we find that answer. Only in He who could say "I am the truth" can we know why we're here.

Recently I viewed a television special on marijuana and youth. It was extremely distressing to me to see these naive, foolish young people throwing their lives away and destroying their bodies in their ignorance. I think particularly of a twelve-year-old boy who was getting stoned morning, noon, and night and had been since he was eight years old. When asked why, he replied that it was simply to enjoy himself, because it felt good. He liked to just sit there and have the feeling of euphoria. So he sat in school all day, though he never heard or understood or learned anything. He came home and sat. He never did anything, never accomplished anything, and will never amount to anything if he continues this way.

Before we condemn that, may I say it's a very mature, intelligent, advanced response to the hedonism of our culture. If life is merely to enjoy, then that young boy is right and there's no answer from secular society that can show he's wrong.

He never did anything, never accomplished anything, and will never amount to anything.

If, on the other hand, we've been created by God and have been placed in this world as a probation...if we've been charged to accomplish certain things and to serve God and our fellow man...if one day we'll give an account of ourselves in the final judgment...if our eternal bliss or punishment is determined by how we live our lives here...then that young man is tragically wrong.

The truth is to be found only in Jesus Christ. Christ gives us the truth about our origin. He tells us the truth about our purpose for life. He tells us the truth about the direction for our lives. Christ tells us how we should live and what kind of standard should guide our lives.

There has never been a time when the whole concept of human ethics and morals has been in such total disarray. New ideas being introduced in medicine and new concepts and philosophies competing for the minds of men have left people in utter confusion about how they should live their lives.

Is life something that can be taken? Can it be aborted? Can it be destroyed? How is it to be conducted? How are we to deal with our fellowman? These questions apart from Jesus Christ and His Word have no answers. Therefore, a society or a nation that fails to find the One who is the incarnate Truth about these matters will be adrift in the maze of relativism, not knowing where it came from or where it's going.

Jesus Christ also tells us the truth about the power to live our lives. We not only need to know how we should live, but we desperately need to have power to live that kind of life. Christ is the only One who can say that He sends His Spirit to come and live in our hearts, to renew us, to regenerate us, and to empower us to live as God would have us live. The truth about the power for living is found in Jesus Christ, and wise men will seek that truth.

Wise men will also seek the truth about their destiny, about where they're going. There's no more consummate fool than the person who lives his life without seriously considering where he's going. I'm continually amazed and astounded by the number of fools who walk abroad in this land,

- acting as if they were going to live forever on this earth;
- never giving more than a moment's contemplation as to what will happen to them eternally;
- planning vastly more for a two-week vacation than for where they'll spend eternity;
- supposing that if they've bought a plot and selected a casket and made out a will, they've prepared for the future.

"But God said to him, 'Fool! This night your soul will be required of you; then whose will those things be?'" (Luke 12:20).

There are so many people wallowing in the mud flats of materialism with sensate cravings for earthly and temporal things, who have never lifted their eyes to the heavens, who don't realize God has made us for eternity. That revelation is to be found in the truth that's in Christ, who has brought to light life and immortality, the One who can tell us He is the truth and He is the way. Christ is the only One who can tell us the truth about how we can arrive at the destiny we all desire so much. Only in Him is that truth to be found.

How shall we find our way to the destiny we desire? Only through faith in Jesus Christ. Only through coming and submitting ourselves to Him as Savior and Lord. Only through trusting in His atoning work rather than in any goodness of our own. Only through faith in Him. This is the way that leads to eternal life. This is our hope.

Those wise men of old followed what little light they had, and it brought them at last into the presence of the living, incarnate God.

Conclusion

Everyone is seeking something in life. I would ask you to consider this question: what are *you* seeking? Do you seek power? Do you seek wealth? Do you seek fame that your name may be remembered? There's nothing wrong with any of those if you seek them in the right way. But seek them in the wrong way, and they're tragically fatal.

However, in Jesus Christ we have wealth untold. In Jesus Christ we shall live forever. In Jesus Christ we have the power of His Spirit, and we say, "I can do all things through Christ who strengthens me" (Philippians 4:13).

11

Running the Race

Let us run with endurance
the race that is set before us.

HEBREWS 12:1

The purpose of life is to glorify God (who's not so hidden after all) and to enjoy Him forever. We're to know Him and make Him known.

What, then, is the Christian life, or to what shall we liken it?

Scripture gives us a number of metaphors. For example, we're told it's a pilgrimage, as John Bunyan elaborated in his classic book, *The Pilgrim's Progress.* Our pilgrimage is from the City of Destruction unto the Celestial City, and *The Pilgrim's Progress* tells us about all the potential bypasses and detours we confront along the way.

We're also told that the Christian life is warfare, that we're wrestling against principalities and powers. We're to put on the whole armor of God. Bunyan developed that theme in *The Holy War,* his great book on the battle for Mansoul.

The author of the book of Hebrews tells us of another metaphor. He says the Christian life is like a race:

Therefore we also, since we are surrounded by so great a
cloud of witnesses, let us lay aside every weight, and the sin

which so easily ensnares us, and let us run with endurance the
race that is set before us. (12:1)

Here is a beautiful portrayal of the Christian life. Scholars say the
picture the writer has in mind is that of the great athletic contests of
those days, like the Olympic Games, which in antiquity were known
throughout the world, as they are today. Here we can imagine the sta-
dium filled with all sorts of spectators and the time arriving for the
great race.

A question comes to mind: is the writer of Hebrews saying that
those believers who have gone before us, who have died and gone to
heaven, are like the serried rows of spectators, rank after rank, in the
great amphitheater watching what is taking place in our race here
below? Are our deceased loved ones and friends and neighbors watching everything we do here in this life?

Such a thought may spur us on to some greater endeavor, and
yet I don't believe that's what the writer really has in mind. The
confusion arises in the word translated as "witnesses." It's from
the Greek word *martyres,* from which we get the word *martyrs.*
The writer is referring back to those mentioned in the previous
chapter, Hebrews 11, the great Hall of Fame chapter about the
men and women of faith in the Old Testament, many of whom
were martyrs: "They were stoned, they were sawn in two, were
tempted, were slain with the sword. They wandered about in
sheepskins and goatskins, being destitute, afflicted, tormented...
They wandered in deserts and mountains, in dens and caves of
the earth" (verses 37–38). They "became valiant in battle, turned
to flight the armies of the aliens" (verse 34). Here was a mighty
group, men and women of great faith. Many gave their lives for

what they believed, and "the world was not worthy" of them, the writer tells us (verse 38).

So the word *martyr* in Greek can mean "one who witnesses something," but its principal meaning is "one who testifies to that which he has experienced." We're called to be witnesses for Christ, which isn't a call to be a spectator but to be an active proclaimer of that which we've personally experienced. So I don't think the scripture here is telling us that those who have preceded us into glory are watching all that takes place on earth. Most theologians would agree on that point.

If they were watching everything here, this would seem to create difficulties. Imagine a woman who is enjoying the perfect felicity and bliss of heaven. How would she feel if she looked to earth and saw her daughter fall into temptation, become overwhelmed with sin, and experience a disastrous calamity in her life? How could a father be completely happy in heaven if he watched his son on earth have a terrible accident and become maimed and disfigured for life? Quite obviously there's a contradiction between observing that which takes place in this world and living in perfect bliss above. So I think the reference is to the fact that we're surrounded by a great cloud of martyrs—those who suffered, who strove, who were valiant in the fight, who in many cases gave their lives for what they believed—and, therefore, we should be motivated by their examples to run the race in a better fashion.

Running a race is serious business.

Running a race is serious business. Running in the Olympics is for some the culmination of lifelong effort. You are surely aware of how grueling is the training and discipline that Olympic athletes must undergo. We see, therefore, that the Christian life also is an earnest affair. It's a *serious* matter, a matter of moment and significance. It will have not only temporal but eternal consequences.

The world tells us in song that "life is just a bowl of cherries," but Scripture says otherwise. That doesn't mean life is all solemn and the corners of our mouths should be turned down and there's no joy or rejoicing or happiness. But many people today need to have a much more serious view of life. We're called to great demands and responsibilities. We're called to bring about the kingdom of God.

We're given a great challenge to win the world for Jesus Christ. Yet most of us in our frivolous pursuit of pleasure, diversions, and amusements are wasting so much of our time, energy, talent, and treasure on things that are mere froth when we should have a more serious view of life.

The ultimate resolution of the great international conflicts in the world today may depend upon which people have the greater and more earnest view of life. If that's the case, what does it say for America? I've often thought that if terrorists attacked our nation during the Super Bowl, we would hardly notice.

BESETTING SIN

Hebrews 12:1 admonishes us: "Lay aside every weight." Some things that aren't sinful in themselves may still be deterrents to running the race. Even though something isn't inherently bad, we may need to put it aside and fix our attention on that which will better help us run the race successfully.

A few years ago coauthor Jerry Newcombe ran a marathon in January in Miami and found that runners along the way would sometimes shed their light jackets and sweatshirts. His friends who have run in colder marathons, such as the one held each November in New York City, find this phenomenon even more pronounced. The morning is cold, but once the runners start moving and warm up, the sweatshirt becomes a liability. Some marathon organizers expect this situation and even have workers who follow the runners and pick up all this discarded clothing to donate to charity. In running a serious race, even a light jacket can hamper the run. How much more so if we're weighed down by something heavy?

Something keeps us from being what we ought to be.

We're also told in that verse to lay aside the "sin which so easily ensnares us." The King James Version refers to this as the sin that does so easily "beset us." The besetting sin is the one that wraps itself around our legs and trips us up and causes us to fall. Any sin can become a besetting sin. Each one of us probably has a particular area, because of our psychological and constitutional makeup, that is a source of temptation and frustration.

What is your besetting sin? Perhaps alcohol is overwhelming your life. Or it may be gluttony. (We don't hear many sermons on gluttony these days, do we?) It may be lust. It may be drug addiction. I've no doubt there are a number of addicts in our churches today. Perhaps it's nicotine, one of the most addictive drugs. Any of these can keep us from being free.

This is a concern that applies to each of us. Something keeps us from being what we ought to be.

Some trees are easy to cut down. You just cut around the root, and the tree falls over. But with other trees, that doesn't seem to affect them at all, because they have a taproot in the center that goes deep into the earth. If you're ever going to get that tree loose, you have to cut the taproot.

What's the taproot that holds you to this world, bringing carnality and worldliness to your life and keeping you from being the mature Christian you ought to be? Is it the love of pleasure? Is it sloth? Is it love of money? What is keeping you down?

Whatever it is, lay it aside and run the race Christ has given you to run.

This race, of course, is not only the picture of the beginning of our Christian life and salvation but the ongoing portrayal of our life and sanctification, as we run with Jesus Christ through the Christian life.

THE SECRET OF THE CHRISTIAN LIFE

How are we to run this race? Where are we to get the strength?

There are some people who get weary just thinking about running a race. How shall we get the energy to run a sustained race, energy that will last throughout our lifetime?

The answer to that—the secret to the strength of the Christian life, even the secret to salvation itself—is found in Hebrews 12:2: "Looking unto Jesus, the author and finisher of our faith." Looking unto Christ, who is the great object of our habitual meditation. This is the secret of the Christian life, both to beginning it and to continuing it.

At age sixteen Charles Spurgeon of England was miserably convicted of his sin and was looking for something he couldn't find. He went into a little church where a layman was preaching a sermon on the text "Look unto me, and be ye saved, all the ends of the earth: for I am God, and there is none else" (Isaiah 45:22, KJV).

The preacher that day looked down at this young visitor in the midst of the twenty or so people present and fixed his eyes on him. "Young man," he said, "you're miserable." Charles Spurgeon couldn't argue with that, though he certainly wasn't used to having a preacher address him directly in a sermon.

The preacher then said, "Young man, you're going to be miserable for all eternity unless you heed and obey my text: 'Look unto me, and be ye saved.'"

So Spurgeon, by a look of faith, was saved in that very hour. And he went on to become perhaps the greatest preacher of all time.

Looking is likened unto faith, and faith is likened unto looking—because a look is easily the simplest thing we can possibly do. Faith is simply looking to the Cross of Christ, as Spurgeon did that day. It's not a huge, strenuous effort. If God told us we had to go outside and climb a flagpole to be saved, I'm sure many would attempt it. If He told us we had to run a marathon, millions in this world would try. If He told us we had to swim the English Channel, people would line up on the beaches.

And yet He tells us we must simply look to Jesus. It's like in the Old Testament, when the camp of the Israelites was invaded by poisonous snakes that were biting and killing them. According to God's instructions, the people took a bronze image of one of the snakes and lifted it atop a pole. To be healed, all the people had to do was look to that snake on the pole, which was a picture of sin being lifted up—even as Christ, who became the sin-bearer of the world, was lifted up so that we may look to Him and see that sin is being dealt with by God in the person of His Son, Jesus Christ.

Just a look is all it takes to be saved.

Just a look is all it takes to be saved. Just a look of faith. As a child looks to his father to meet his deepest needs, as a person who is ill looks to the physician for healing, so we look to Jesus Christ not only at the beginning for our salvation but also throughout the whole of the Christian life.

In the Greek text, this "looking" is a present participle, indicating a continuous looking unto Jesus rather than just a hasty glance—like some frenetic tourist rushing through the Louvre to view hundreds of paintings in a half hour or so. What's taught in Hebrews 12 is more like sitting down in front of Christ as one would sit down in front of a beautiful painting, not simply quickly glancing and then looking away but letting the loveliness soak in until every color and every tint and every hue and every tinge is absorbed into one's very soul and becomes a part of the experience.

So we're to look to Christ—not just in a fleeting moment or two in the morning or before bedtime, but consistently so that His personality, His moral purity, His strength, His love, and His grace might flow into us and change us.

The Antidote to Sin

Scripture admonishes us to look unto Jesus as "the author and finisher of our faith" (Hebrews 12:2). He's the sole and single antidote to all sin.

Are you tempted? Look to Jesus, for He "was in all points tempted as we are, yet without sin" (Hebrews 4:15).

Have you been treated wrongly? Has your heart grown hard and bitter because of the things done and said to you? "Consider Him who endured such hostility from sinners against Himself" (Hebrews 12:3).

Do you find it difficult to forgive those who have done you badly? Remember the startling words He spoke to those who had just completed His crucifixion: "Father, forgive them, for they do not know what they do" (Luke 23:34).

Sit down in front of Jesus and let His purity, peace, love, mercy, compassion, truth, and holiness seep into your soul. Consider Him until you see Him in all His beauty, sharply delineated. It's one of the wonders of the world that Christ stands out so clearly to the eye of faith today.

Consider how the gathering mists of oblivion have swirled around and hidden the faces of the other great names of antiquity until they stand now merely as poor, pale phantoms. Contrast that with the warm, solid hand of Christ reaching out to clasp the hands of those who trust in Him. How solid and real and inspiring He is today.

The Greek verb for "looking unto Jesus" is unusual. It's a compound verb that contains the meaning of looking *away* from one thing in order to closely view another. What should we look away *from*? We must look away from ourselves. This is the essence of faith. Faith is finally looking away from ourselves unto Christ. It means we must look away from our own sins, which bring despair and hopelessness, and gaze instead at Jesus Christ.

EXCEEDING JOY

The final thing to consider here is a word that has touched me deeply since I first grasped its meaning. In fact, when I first understood what it meant, it brought tears to my eyes, as it has on several occasions since.

We read in Hebrews 12:2 that Jesus "endured the cross, despising the shame" and that He did this "for the *joy* that was set before Him."

I remember wondering as a young Christian what joy could possibly have been set before Christ that could have made Him willing to endure the piercing agony, the unbelievable pain and suffering of the cross. What joy could that be?

Then there came to me the words of a biblical benediction:

Now to Him who is able to keep you from stumbling, and to present you faultless before the presence of His glory *with exceeding joy,* to God our Savior, who alone is wise, be glory and majesty. (Jude 24–25)

What joy? The joy of presenting you and me *faultless* before the presence of His glory.

On that great Judgment Day, before angels and archangels, cherubim and seraphim, before the multitudes gathered from every nation, tongue, and tribe upon this earth, Jesus Christ will present us cleansed by His precious blood. By His doing, we'll be clothed in His perfect white righteousness, in His own obedience, faultless before His glory with *exceeding joy.*

I don't know about you, but that touches my heart. For that joy—the joy of presenting me, Jim Kennedy, faultless before the throne of God—our Jesus endured the cross, despising the shame. He placed His shoulder beneath that cross and placed His foot upon the shame, despising it.

There are many people who would rather suffer physical torture than to suffer shame, to be humiliated, laughed at, mocked, and ridiculed. Yet Jesus took all this for the joy of presenting us faultless before His Father.

CONCLUSION

That joy will be *our* experience—if we run with patience the race set before us, looking daily, hourly, and moment by moment to Jesus, the Author and Finisher of our faith.

May we finish the race…and receive the crown.

Luther's Quest for God

You will find Him if you seek Him
with all your heart and with all your soul.
Deuteronomy 4:29

D uring different stages of church history, God seems sometimes to be hidden. That is to say, He's sometimes obscured
by teaching that goes beyond the simple gospel.

Currently, among many mainstream Protestants (not evangeli-
cals), there's a greater commitment to whatever liberal cause comes
down the pike than there is to the historic Christian faith. Rather
than knowing and proclaiming God, who has revealed Himself in
Jesus Christ, they obscure God's revelation and often teach the opposite of what He has revealed in His Word. They might as well call
their congregations The Church of What's Happening Now.

There's bitter irony in this, because Protestantism began at a time
when there was also a great deal of obscuring of God's truth and
therefore obscuring God from the people.

LUTHER'S DISCOVERY

I want to turn your attention to Martin Luther's rediscovery of the
simple gospel. It came at a time when God's presence was being hidden

by false doctrine in the church. Luther provides a perpetual reminder of the need for the light of the gospel to shine forth in a dark culture, for it sparked a tremendous spiritual revival.

Martin Luther has been dearly loved and dearly hated.

Martin Luther has been dearly loved and dearly hated. There are those who have sung his praises and those who excoriated him. What shall we say about him? What kind of a man was Martin Luther? The late pope John Paul II praised Luther as being a "profoundly religious man," an appraisal of Luther that "generally reflects Catholic thinking today," according to the late Reverend John F. Hotchkin, an ecumenical leader in the Roman Catholic Church.[1]

REVISED THOUGHTS ON LUTHER

Indeed, there has been a tremendous transformation in the opinion of many people concerning Martin Luther. You may know that for a few decades now, Lutherans and Roman Catholics had been involved in a colloquy, which they concluded not long ago, and have released their findings—findings that startled much of the world. *Christianity Today,* as well as many news magazines, described the conclusions:

> Father Tavard [of the Roman Catholic Church] says that "today many Catholic scholars think Luther was right in his central doctrine of justification by faith and the [sixteenth-century Catholic] church was blind to the point he was making." He observes that "both Lutherans and Catholics agree that good works by Christian believers are the result of their faith and the working of divine grace in them, not their per-

sonal contributions to their own salvation. Christ is the only Savior. One does not save oneself."[2]

This is a remarkable statement, because that's precisely what Luther was revealing to the world some five hundred years ago.

Not only has the Catholic Church revised its thinking about the monk Martin Luther, but even the communists did so in the waning days of the Soviet bloc. In 1983 a committee was formed to arrange a monumental celebration for this great German hero on the five hundredth anniversary of his birth on November 10, 1483, in the town of Eisleben, Saxony, which was part of communist East Germany for several decades after World War II.. Who was the leader of that committee? It was none other than Erich Honecker, the East German communist leader.

Will Durant said of Luther's translations of the Old and New Testaments: "These translations were epochal events. They inaugurated German literature.... His translation...is still the greatest prose work in the national literature."[3]

THE GOSPEL OF GRACE

Many years ago I stood in the city of Worms (pronounced "Vorms") in the courtyard of that city's huge Catholic cathedral. A plaque on the ground was engraved with these words in German: "Here stood Martin Luther for God and country." Of course, Luther stood for the gospel of Jesus Christ, which had, unfortunately, been forgotten.

We should, however, remember that the gospel of grace was first revealed by God to Abraham. (It had even been revealed to Adam, but it was revealed more fully to Abraham.) Jesus Christ said, "Abraham rejoiced to see My day, and he saw it and was glad" (John 8:56).

The gospel of His grace was revealed nineteen hundred years before Jesus was born, but by the time Christ came, alas, it had been covered over with the legalism and the various works of the Pharisees and the rituals thereof. It was lost except to a very few, but Christ came to earth and brought it to light again.

Then this gospel went out and changed the world. But centuries later, it again became overlaid with superstition, legalism, and human rituals, until by the Middle Ages it had been obscured once more.

It was then that this humble monk at Wittenberg once more discovered and revealed to the world the gospel of grace, resulting in the tremendous spiritual revival that transformed the face of Europe and much of the world.

It took Protestants less than five hundred years to lose the doctrine of justification.

I venture to say that today not one Protestant in four could give the faintest explanation of the doctrine of justification. The church is desperately in need of a reformation. The Protestant church is desperately in need of another Martin Luther. Note well, it took the Jews nineteen hundred years to lose it. It took the Catholics fifteen hundred years to lose it. But it took the Protestants less than five hundred years to lose it. We have little of which to boast.

THE DOCTRINE OF JUSTIFICATION

The doctrine of justification is the very center of the Christian faith. The great historical theologian Dr. Edward Boehl says that the entire Protestant Reformation moved on the lever of justification by faith. This, he says, is the core of Christian doctrine, the kernel of saving truth, and the axle on which moves the entire chariot of salvation. It's the *only* key to heaven.

John Calvin said that the doctrine of justification by faith is the article of a standing or a failing church. How true that is. It's the doctrine that answers the question asked by Job forty centuries ago: how shall a sinful person ever stand in the presence of an all-holy God? That's precisely the question Martin Luther wrestled with and agonized over so manfully. How indeed?

Sad to say, in our day very few people are consciously wrestling with that question, because we've answered it in a simple fashion. We've simply done away with sin, having transmuted it into neuroses and psychoses. We've also done away with an all-holy God, having turned Him into an all-loving grandfather who wouldn't think of punishing His children.

The very thought of a God who cannot even look upon sin and who has promised to visit our transgressions with the rod is beyond the pale of thinking for the average person. So having transformed both sin and God in this way, man is no longer seeking acceptance with God; rather, he simply seeks an appointment with the psychiatrist. Having assuaged his feelings of guilt, he supposes that all is well with him and the world. But is it?

What did Luther discover? What is justification? What does it mean?

If you don't understand it—at least the rudimentary teaching, if not the theological jargon—it's the gospel; it's the glad tidings; it's that which the angels sang about on that first Christmas morn when their leader said, "I bring you good tidings of great joy" (Luke 2:10).

The doctrine of justification is simply this. Righteousness is not our gift to God but God's gift to us. Righteousness isn't something we work up by our own strivings and piety and morality and then offer to God at the Judgment Day. Rather, the only righteousness acceptable to God is that perfect righteousness wrought by His own dear Son, Jesus Christ, the only One who could say of God the Father, "I always do those things that please Him" (John 8:29). The perfect life of Christ and His atoning death make up the essence of the white robe of pure righteousness with which we stand faultless before the throne of God.

LUTHER'S PILGRIMAGE

What led Luther to rediscover the doctrine of justification by faith alone? Let's take a look at his pilgrimage.

Luther was born of humble parents. His father was a miner who saved his money all his life to send his son to the University of Erfurt to study law. Martin had a brilliant record in college. His father felt he was going to make a fine lawyer.

One day, after visiting his family, Luther and a friend started on their trek across the countryside to go back to the city and the university. A storm overtook them, and the clouds threatened. As they reached the crest of a hill, there was a tremendous crash, and lightning struck right at Luther's feet, instantly killing his friend and throwing Luther on his face in the mud. He turned and looked heavenward. His smitten conscience could see the specter of death, judgment, and condemnation in hell.

His smitten conscience could see the specter of death, judgment, and condemnation in hell.

Perhaps he could make a "deal" with God, so Luther called on the mother of Mary to help him in this moment of his absolute terror and dread: "Help, Saint Anne, and I will enter a monastery."

So into a monastery he went. And as the monastery doors clanged shut behind him, Martin Luther was dead to the world. He cared not one whit for anything that transpired on this planet. Only one concern absorbed his every waking moment and thought and all his energy, and that was the salvation of his own soul. How could he, a sinful man, ever be able to stand in the presence of an infinitely holy God, who was a consuming fire?

He gave himself completely to the task. He prayed three hours every day. He confessed his sins hour after hour to the confessors, who finally hated to see him coming. He would flagellate himself with a whip and be found unconscious, in a pool of blood, by his fellow monks in the morning. He fasted day after day. Once he prayed continually for six weeks without eating, and only every three or four days would he sleep for an hour or two. He would stay out all night long, naked, in the deep German snow, trying to purify his soul, trying to make himself acceptable in the sight of a God who knows no sin. But *it was all in vain.*

Do you hear me, you poor imitation of Luther, you who think that by your poor, faint, pitiful works you are going to earn your way into heaven? Take a lesson from a man who really made a go at it. At the end of it all, Luther said, "Love God? I hated him!"[4]

But before you judge Luther too harshly, may I suggest you stay out all night, naked, in deep snow. And pray for six weeks, without eating, to get right with God. Then, having found no peace in your troubled soul, pronounce your condemnation on poor Monk Martin.

"The Just Shall Live by Faith"

The monastery eventually sent him to Rome as an emissary. Luther's heart leaped at the prospects. When he saw on the horizon the Holy City of Rome, he was filled with anticipation. He ran, he said, like a mad pilgrim, from one church to another, from one shrine to another, from one Mass to another. But he noticed that while he was saying one Mass, his fellow priests were saying four or five. In fact, they said to him, *"Passa. Passa,"* meaning "Get a move on." They also told him that if there was a hell, Rome was built upon it. It was a city filled with vice and immorality. Some of the priests even boasted of their virtue in that they had sex only with females.

Luther was undaunted. He made his way to the *Scala Sancta* in the Lateran church. The huge stairs—the stairs that tradition says led up to the throne of Pontius Pilate—had been brought from Jerusalem. On them Jesus Christ had stood, scourged, flogged, almost stripped of His very skin by the Romans, and clothed in a purple robe, His blood dripping on those stairs as He was turned over to the mob to be crucified. (Those stairs, with bloodstains now covered with glass, are still in Rome. I've seen them.)

Luther began to climb those stairs on his knees, kissing each stair and saying his rosary. He reached halfway up this long flight of marble stairs. Then the word he'd first seen in the epistle to the Romans…the word that became, as Luther said, the very gate to paradise…the word that is the birth text of the Protestant church…that word God began to speak to him again. He'd come across it with complete bewilderment: "As it is written, 'The just shall live by faith'" (Romans 1:17). (That phrase—"The just shall live by faith"—is found in the Old Testament and again three times in the New Testament.)

Luther was completely mystified by it. What did it mean? He couldn't understand it.

He continued up the stairs on his knees, and God began to speak to him with that word again. At first it was *pianissimo:* "Dear Martin, the just shall live by faith." It became *forte:* "The just shall live by faith!" Then it seemed to resound throughout all the room, throughout the church, and throughout the whole world: "THE JUST SHALL LIVE BY FAITH!"

Suddenly Luther's eyes were opened. He leaped to his feet, and finally he saw—he saw the gospel. He saw the truth. He saw the grace of God. He saw that a person is justified by faith, that those who are justified by faith in the blood of Christ are those who will live, and that those who seek to justify themselves in any other way shall not live.

Suddenly Luther's eyes were opened.

Luther ran down the stairs. He made his way back to Wittenberg and began to proclaim the good news: *righteousness is a gift of God wrought by Christ, received by faith.* Take heart, good friend, God is gracious and merciful, as well as just and holy.

Before long these words, which spread all over Germany and Europe by means of the newly invented printing press, met with some who didn't take to them too kindly. Others declared them to be heresy—indeed, the same "heresy" Jan Hus had proclaimed years before, and the same heresy proclaimed by John Wycliffe in England as well.

LUTHER DEBATES ECK

Luther went to debate the great theologian Johann Eck, and in that debate this incredibly learned man was totally bested by Luther, who used Scripture as a sword that could not be broken.

Luther was called to the Diet of Worms to account for himself. His friends told him, "Do not go. Remember Jan Hus." A hundred years earlier the Bohemian professor and preacher Jan Hus had proclaimed the same doctrine. He'd been invited to the Council of Constance to "discuss" his teachings and to debate the points at issue. He was granted safe passage and made his way there. When he arrived, Hus was asked one question: "Will you recant?" No opportunity for debate. No discussion. Simply, "Recant or burn." Kindling sticks were gathered around him and lighted, and Jan Hus went up in smoke.

"Remember Jan Hus," Luther was told. "Do not go to Worms. You'll be killed."

Luther answered, "Though the devils be as thick as the tiles upon the roof, I will go," and so he made his way across the country to the imperial city of Worms. Tens of thousands of people were there, having heard that Monk Martin, the hero of Germany, was going to meet with Charles V, ruler of the Holy Roman Empire—a most spectacular event.

Luther was ushered into a gigantic hall, where five thousand people had gathered. At the end of the hall, on a great throne chair, sat the young, newly crowned emperor Charles V. Beside him were Eck and other representatives from the pope in Rome. Around the room were princes and dukes, knights and barons, archbishops and cardinals, and officials of every kind.

Luther was led out in his humble monk's apparel. In the center of the room was a long table on which were spread some twenty different books. Eck would hear no more. Luther was warned not to speak unless he was questioned, and he was asked these questions:

One, "Are these your books?"

Luther looked them over and said, "Yes, these are my books."

Two, "Will you recant?"

Hus all over again, thought Luther. No opportunity for debate. No opportunity for discussion.

Luther's knees grew weak. His face became pale. Finally he said in a soft and weak voice, "Since the issue at stake here is the eternal salvation of human souls, I request some time to consider the matter."

The crowd began to jeer. Some of the Spaniards mocked him with hisses as he was led out of the room.

Luther prayed all that night. The next morning he was once more led back into the great assembly hall. Once more thousands were gathered inside and tens of thousands outside. Once more he was brought to the center table, and again he was asked by Eck, "Will you recant?"

Luther, strengthened now by the Spirit of God, replied, "As you can see, some of these books are on subjects such as the Lord's Prayer, which are held in common by all, and some on issues on which there is no controversy."

Eck would hear no more of this. He grew impatient and said, "We will have an answer without horns. Tell us roundly and frankly, will you or will you not recant?"

LUTHER'S COURAGEOUS STAND

The moment of crisis had come. The entire future of religious liberty now stood in the garment of one poor monk. His conscience saturated with the Word of God, both in German and in Latin, Luther uttered these words:

> Unless I am refuted and convicted by the testimonies of the Scriptures or by clear arguments (since I believe neither the Pope nor the councils alone; it being evident that they have often erred and contradicted themselves), I am conquered by the Holy Scriptures quoted by me, and my conscience is bound in the word of God: I can not and will not recant any thing, since it is unsafe and dangerous to do any thing against the conscience.[5]

Uproar. Pandemonium. People cried out, "Heretic! Burn him!" Eck said to Luther, "You cannot prove it." Luther said he would, if given a chance. Finally Eck's voice was heard again: "Will you recant?"

With the flames around the stake appearing before his eyes, Luther then said the words that have most clearly etched themselves in the conscience of Christians through the centuries: "On this I take my stand. I can do no other. God help me."

He was given twenty days by the emperor to recant or be burned, but before the time was up, he was kidnapped by his friends and taken to Wartburg Castle. There, in hiding, he translated the Scriptures into German, which transformed not only that people's religion but also their literature and language.

The truth and the struggle that were Luther's are the only hope we have.

The word of the gospel continued to go out and spread all the way around the world, until we come to this day when those on both sides of the issue now know that what Luther said was true. As one Catholic theologian said after the Second Vatican Council in 1962–65, "Luther got the council he asked for, but 450 years too late."[6]

The truth and the struggle that were Luther's are the only hope we have. Everyone struggles with the same question: "How shall a sinful man stand in the presence of a holy God?"

CONCLUSION

Despite all the naysaying of modernity, God is still holy, sin is still sin, and the judgment hastens on apace. We'll all stand, not before the Holy Roman Emperor, but before the Lord God Almighty, who sees into every heart and knows every thought and every word and every deed. We shall indeed struggle then, if not now, with this question: how shall a sinful person stand in the presence of a holy God?

Luther's answer to the question (in his Shorter Catechism) rings through the centuries: God out of His grace forgives us our sins, imparts to us the righteousness of Christ, and looks at us, through Him, as if we'd never sinned.

PART IV

SHADOWS
THAT SEEM TO
OBSCURE GOD

Doubts About God

For now we see in a mirror, dimly,
but then face to face.
Now I know in part,
but then I shall know
just as I also am known.
1 CORINTHIANS 13:12

The thrust of this book's message is that God is no longer hidden, since He has revealed Himself so clearly in Jesus Christ our Lord. But what about the Christian who feels God is far from him? What about the Christian for whom God seems hidden? The idea of a hidden God even comes from Isaiah, a Hebrew prophet who was very close to the Lord: "Truly You are God, who hide Yourself, O God of Israel, the Savior!" (Isaiah 45:15).

In this chapter we'll explore doubts that sometimes seem to obscure God and how those doubts relate to our sufferings and to our prayers.

Honest doubt is no sin. The greatest human being, according to Jesus, was John the Baptist. However, while he languished in prison, he sent word to Jesus reflecting his doubts. He essentially asked Jesus if He was the One to come or if there was someone else yet to come. Jesus gently rebuked him by saying, "Blessed is he who is not offended because of Me" (Matthew 11:6).

UNANSWERED PRAYERS

There are several things that can hide the face of God from us. One of them is unanswered prayers, and that may be caused by unconfessed sin, disobedience, and other things we've done to move away from God. God could be testing us and forming us into His image by periods of silence from heaven. If our prayers seem to just bounce off the ceiling, if they seem to be no longer answered, perhaps God is trying to get our attention about something.

If there's a key to answered prayer, and I'm sure there is, it could be nothing other than praying as God would have us pray. For only as our prayers fit with God's purposes for our lives will there be any hope of their being answered. The solution is to pray according to His will. For example, we can pray according to the pattern and the words Jesus taught us in the Lord's Prayer—with praise of God, confession of sin, requests for our needs and for strength to resist sin, and closing in praise of God.

AN UNFRIENDLY UNIVERSE?

Another manifestation of doubt we may experience is something we borrow from the worldly culture around us. Many modern unbelievers look out into the vastness of the universe and ask the question: is the universe friendly? I can't vouch for the universe; surely the jungle is red in tooth and claw, and there are many dangerous things in this fallen universe. But one thing I know beyond any doubt: He who created it is far beyond friendly. He loves us with an everlasting love, and He has promised He will take care of us.

When it gets right down to it, all of us, no matter how mature we may be, no matter what success we may have achieved, really want to know there's a mommy or a daddy who will take care of us when things get rough. Eventually mommies and daddies leave this world, but wonder of wonders, the Great Father in heaven will take care of us, and He is able to take care of us far better than an earthly parent ever could.

No one can go through this life without sorrow, pain, and hard, seemingly unanswerable questions.

Virtually no person can go through this life without times of sorrow, pain, and hard, seemingly unanswerable questions. But throughout this life, no matter what difficulties come our way, He'll transform them for our good, even the great tragedy of death itself.

OTHER GODS AND RELIGIONS

Another frequent cause for doubt is the plethora of other religions around us. In our global village we're exposed to many other religious views and other gods, particularly the gods from the East. Are they real? Are they false? What should we think? Some people have said, "Well, there's really just one religion with different faces, and we're all basically going to the same God through different paths." That idea was a way to tone down conflicts between various religions.

But then people began to look at other religions a bit more carefully. They discovered more about these three in particular: Islam, Hinduism, and Buddhism.

- Islam is a radical, monotheistic religion. It believes definitely in only one god and makes no room in that unitary god for the Christian Trinity.

- By contrast, in Hinduism there are anywhere from 300,000 to 3,000,000 gods. Nobody really knows for sure.
- Meanwhile, in Buddhism there's no god at all, at least for most Buddhists. Some have tried to make a god out of Buddha, but for the most part, they're skeptical of God's existence, as was Buddha himself.

In 1993 at the Parliament of the World's Religions in Chicago, six thousand people from all over the world gathered to try to straighten out the mess, solve the problem, and figure out just what was really going on. After weeks of study they released their paper to explain about God and religion.

If you read that paper, you'll notice something strange: the words *God* or *gods* are never mentioned. You see, the Buddhist priests in attendance wouldn't allow it, because they don't believe in one God or many. They said, "When we pray, we're just meditating. It's psychology, and the only person who hears our prayers is we ourselves."

So what was the solution? There was none. All the conferees did was come up with some ethical suggestions. So religion had dissolved entirely, leaving nothing but ethics at the Parliament of the World's Religions. Isn't that ironic? The parliament was the death knell of this idea that all religions are basically the same. That option just doesn't remain open to any rational being.

Chicago pastor and author Erwin Lutzer attended that Parliament of the World's Religions. He noted, "The Scriptures require us to view other religions as the flawed attempts of man to reach God through human effort and insight."[1] As you may recall, Jesus says in the gospel of John, "All who ever came before Me are thieves and robbers.... The thief does not come except to steal, and to kill.... I am the good shepherd. The good shepherd gives His life for the sheep" (John 10:8, 10–11). No one else except Jesus has laid down his life for the sheep. So Christ says that these others are not gods by any means.

Some today say we should bow down and reverence all these other religions. But the apostle Paul asserted that heathen peoples sacrificed to demons and not to God, and he added, "I do not want you to have fellowship with demons" (1 Corinthians 10:20). This is certainly the view held all the way through the Old Testament.

What was the attitude of Elijah on Mount Carmel toward the false prophets, the prophets of the pagan god Baal, who showed themselves to be false prophets? Didn't Elijah command that they be destroyed? (See 1 Kings 18:17–40.)

Or what was the Bible teaching us about Dagon, the Philistine fish-god, which fell flat on its face in its own temple when the captured ark of the Lord was placed there? (See 1 Samuel 5:1–4.)

How about Molech, that detestable Semitic god to whom idolatrous Israelites once made sacrifices right outside the walls of Jerusalem? They had a gigantic, hollow metal image of Molech. On certain festival occasions they would build a bonfire inside the image until it glowed red hot. Into its fiery, outstretched hands they would place their babies and then beat louder on the drums in an effort to drown out their babies' cries. What was the Bible teaching us about that? (See Leviticus 20:2.)

> This place of worship for a pagan god is the place Jesus chose as a description of hell.

By the way, when the Jews finally destroyed that place of Molech, they made it into the garbage heap of Jerusalem. It's in the of Valley of Hinnom—*gê hinnöm* in Hebrew, and *Gehenna* in Greek, which became one of the words for "hell." So this place of worship for one of the pagan gods of this world is a place Jesus chose as a description of hell—hardly an attitude of reverence.

Dr. Charles Hodge, a nineteenth-century professor at Princeton Theological Seminary and one of the greatest of American theologians, wrote this:

> Men of the world do not intend to serve Satan, when they
> break the laws of God in the pursuit of their objects of desire.
> Still in so doing they are really obeying the will of the great
> adversary, yielding to his impulses, and fulfilling his designs.
> He is therefore said to be the god of this world. To him all sin
> is an offering and an homage. We are shut up to the necessity
> of worshipping God or Satan.[2]

This view is our only option concerning other gods. There are thousands of varieties of pagan religions, but they all really boil down to one: the worship of Satan. Of course, I'm excluding Christianity, which is by far the largest religion in the world. It's not really "religion" in the truest sense of the word. It's a *relationship* between God and the people He has called to Himself. But in all pagan religions there is one underlying reality: people are worshiping without knowing that these demons are fallen angels. All their efforts, always, are their own attempts to bring about their own salvation.

The two great questions asked by religion are "Who is God?" and "How can I be with Him forever?" The issues are God and salvation. All pagan religions boil down to man's effort to save himself, so the worship is given to the creature. (By the way, this is also true of some distortions of Christianity, where salvation is essentially by works.) All their hopes are built upon their efforts to save themselves, as opposed to building on Christ, who has proved Himself to be the living God by His resurrection from the dead.

So at three in the morning, when you lie awake and nothing makes sense, remember that Christianity is built on the bedrock of Christ's resurrection, and since that's true, everything else is as well— the authority of the Bible, the deity and humanity of Jesus, and our forgiveness through His sacrificial death for our sins.

DOUBTS FROM SUFFERING

There was a man who was training for the ministry, and his young daughter became ill. His prayers for her recovery went unanswered (or so it seemed). She died, and the man became embittered toward God and the church. He never again pursued the ministry. Instead, he pursued a way to explain the universe as if there were no God. The would-be minister's name was Charles Darwin, who gave atheists a way to explain the universe without God.

Coauthor Jerry Newcombe has a Unitarian friend who's quite honest with him. He has told Jerry on numerous occasions that many Unitarians grew up in destructive church situations and in their childhood experienced some sort of abusive situation. Maybe they were whacked over the head with a yardstick by a nun in grade school. Perhaps their Baptist or Pentecostal parents were overly strict. Some have true horror stories to report. There are many people today who are emotionally embittered by the church and claim to be atheists. Jerry's Unitarian friend has said these people need therapy, as opposed to just going to a Unitarian church, where they essentially seek a religion without God.

I heard about another man who is bitter toward God, whom he denies even exists. He's strongly secular and anti-Christian in every way. He once confided that in his childhood school days, a nun repeatedly berated him in front of the class. She whacked his hand over and over to the point that he bled. To this day he hates God (if there is one) and wants nothing to do with Jesus Christ. What a tragedy. Surely that nun will be held accountable for what she did. Meanwhile, this man goes through life assuming that God (whom he claims not to believe in) is his sworn enemy. The love of God, as seen through Jesus's death on the cross for our sakes, has never penetrated his hard heart. How tragic.

Doubtless many people today are hurting from abusive situations in the church. Stories abound. Such people often have an obscured view of God. This is a great calamity. But it's not just what happens to us that's important. How we react is critically important as well. These same people have also had many positive experiences in their lives. This too is from the hand of God, but they don't acknowledge Him or give Him thanks.

> By refusing to let go and refusing to forgive, they allow their vision of God to be obscured.

Some adults are going through life embittered because they cling to memories of true or perceived injustices from their childhood. By refusing to let go and refusing to forgive, they allow their vision of God to be obscured.

THE EFFECT OF A FATHER

Did you know that our image of God is often shaped by our image of our father? Dr. Paul Vitz, former professor of psychology at New York University (my alma mater), wrote a book entitled *Faith of the Fatherless*. It could just as well be called *The Lack of Faith of the Fatherless*. On the dust jacket of the book, the publishers summarize the message:

Despite its pretensions to cool-headed rationality, modern atheism originated in the irrational, often neurotic, psychological needs of a few powerfully influential thinkers. The psychologist Paul Vitz subjects the apostles of atheism to the same psychological analysis with which they attempted to debunk religious belief. The psychological source of their militant atheism, he shows, was the absence of a good father.[3]

Dr. Vitz looks at the fifteen most influential atheists of the last four centuries and finds that in every case there was either an absent father, a dead father, an abusive father, or a completely incompetent father. This, of course, isn't the only source of atheism, nor is it inevitably the source, but it's a major source.

So you, too, can raise a child to become a Nietzsche, a Sartre, or a Camus. Step one is to ensure your children are raised in a fatherless home.

As an example, Dr. Vitz points out Bertrand Russell, the best-known British atheist of the twentieth century and author of *Why I Am Not a Christian*. He constantly attacked the Christian faith and the Christian God and believers in Christ. What was his upbringing like? His father died when Bertrand was three years old. He loved his father, and after his father died, he was sent to live with a grandfather. A couple of years later, his grandfather died, and he was brought up by his grandmother, Lady Russell, who was known as the "Deadly Nightshade." This woman became the only parental influence he really ever had. And being angry at his father and grandfather for having the temerity to die on him, he expressed this anger eloquently in his hatred for the God and Father of us all.

Jean-Paul Sartre was the most famous French atheist of the twentieth century. His father, Jean Baptiste Sartre, died when young

Jean-Paul was only fifteen months old. A scholar who studied Sartre's life said that after the death of Jean-Paul's father, he lived with his mother and without any significant male role model. She finally remarried, but Jean-Paul had a hostile relationship with his stepfather, which again fits the pattern Dr. Vitz describes. Sartre would later recognize that being fatherless was the cause of his atheism. As he himself said, "If one discards God the father, there has to be someone to invent values.... It's up to you to give [life] a meaning."[4]

Much the same is true for French atheist and existentialist Albert Camus, who said that the only philosophical question worth considering today is suicide. His entire life was spent in a search for a father. His father died when Albert was just one year old, and he grew to feel that absence greatly. He was angry with the Father in heaven for taking his father, and he showed that by his life. Paul Vitz writes, "A melancholy search for his father runs through [*The First Man*] this last and strangely autobiographical work."[5]

Perhaps the most famous atheist in history was someone we looked at earlier, the German philosopher Friedrich Nietzsche, who is best known for the phrase "God is dead." Nietzsche said, "I have absolutely no knowledge of atheism as an outcome of reasoning."[6] It was simply the result of his own experience in life. His father, a Lutheran pastor, died when Nietzsche was four years old. Nietzsche loved his father, and his father tried to love him, but he was sickly. For a year he was mostly bedridden. This was the greatest disaster of young Nietzsche's life. Though he loved his father, he looked upon him as incompetent because he was weak and lacked the "life force."[7]

He rejected God because his own Christian faith lacked that "life force."

If you've read Nietzsche, you know that he uses this term *life force* all the time. That was what he was seeking, and he projected this search onto Christ and Christianity and determined that they lacked "life force." Therefore, he rejected God as a true God because his own Christian faith lacked that "life force." He did not recognize that Jesus Christ is life and life abundant to all those who trust in Him. Finally, Nietzsche had a complete breakdown, and the world's greatest atheist spent his last years in an institution for the insane.

In every case of these atheists, either the father's absence or the father's incompetence impacted the children. They didn't *have* to become atheists, as Dr. Vitz makes clear. They could have decided to turn to God for consolation. But they chose instead to reject Him.

The most modern of the atheists, and the best known in America during the last half of the twentieth century, was Madalyn Murray O'Hair, the woman who succeeded in getting prayer banned from our public schools in the 1960s. Of course, she's no longer in the land of the living because one of her employees, a former felon, killed her.

She often hired parolees, because if they didn't toe the line, she could turn them in and have them sent back to prison. But this particular man had other ideas. He stole nearly $600,000 she'd gathered from American atheists and kidnapped O'Hair and one of her sons and her granddaughter. They all disappeared and were found years later, dismembered.

Her other son, by the way, became a Christian. He is a fascinating man, and we have had him in our home for dinner. In his autobiography he says he remembers clearly the time O'Hair attempted to kill her father with a butcher knife. She failed, but she screamed, "I'll see you dead. I'll get you yet. I'll walk on your grave!"[8] Now that's not what you call a loving relationship with your father. The result: she became a virulent atheist.

Yes, indeed, an absentee father or a brutish father or an abusive father or a weak father—all have an enormous impact upon their children. Scientists have discovered that godly, faithful fathers have an influence and an importance vastly greater than anyone previously imagined. We fathers can have a decisive impact on whether God is "hidden" or clearly seen by our children.

THE SHADOW OF DEATH

Another inducement to doubt that can cause God to seem hidden to some, even devout Christians, is the sense of being threatened by the shadow of death.

A man was walking along the sidewalk with his little girl. She was looking down at the sidewalk when a dark shadow overwhelmed them. With alarm she said, "Daddy, the truck ran over us."

"No, darling," he replied. "That wasn't the truck; it was just the truck's shadow."

Death is the king of terrors, but God's Word teaches us to say this: "Though I walk through the valley of the shadow of death, I will fear no evil" (Psalm 23:4). For it isn't death that hits us; it's only the shadow. Actual death is what hit Christ, and now for us, because of Christ's victory over it, death has lost its power.

Wherever there's a shadow, there's also light, and Christ, the Light of the world, is with us, even in the shadow of death.

Would you know the secret of life? Trust in Christ. Refuse to listen to the whisperings of the devil in those winds that are ever flying around your dwelling, and trust in Jesus Christ.

William Gladstone, a great prime minister of England, had an embroidered plaque mounted on the wall at the foot of his bed. It was the first thing he noticed when he awoke each day and the last thing he saw each night. In spite of the stresses of life as the leader of a great nation, he found peace in its words: "Thou wilt keep him in perfect peace, whose mind is stayed on thee: because he trusteth in thee" (Isaiah 26:3, KJV).

The great truth of this verse is repeated from various angles in hundreds of other texts. It's all there because God wants us to learn *the one most important lesson of all—simply to trust Him.* As has been said, "Earth has no problem that heaven cannot heal."

> We need to trust Him, rest in His promises, and not doubt.

We need to trust Him, rest in His promises, and not doubt. It was through the door of doubt that sin and misery first entered the world, as Satan cast his doubts into the heart and mind of Eve: "Has God indeed said…" (Genesis 3:1). Faith reverses the tempter's whining negation; faith speaks up and says, "Yes, God *has* said!" Thus faith speaks, and *there* faith rests.

The Bible declares, "The just shall live by faith" (Romans 1:17). That's the great secret, the most important secret of successful living.

THE SECRET TO OVERCOMING DOUBTS

The great secret God is trying to teach us—whether about the world which is to come or the world that is now—is that we're to trust in Him for both. If we do, we'll find the secret of living in each. If we do not, we'll forever fail to make that discovery.

At times you may find life overwhelming. You look down the road of your life and see that it's filled with all sorts of fears, impending disasters, tragedies. It seems as though nothing is going to work out right. As you clearly and realistically look at the real world, nothing looks encouraging, so you're troubled with many things. You're distraught.

But remember: "The just shall live by faith" (Romans 1:17). Here is the solution for troubles, for despair, for despondency, and for hopelessness. In this text there's the brightness of an everlasting hope.

It seems that Satan has two principal enticements for people. On the one hand he says, "Come and do it my way. Forget about God. Try it this way. Live for the pleasures of the flesh. You only go around once; grab all the gusto you can."

If that doesn't work, and you persist in your walk with God, what does Satan do next? He yells, "Look out! Calamity! The bridge is out. Disaster ahead. Everything's going to pieces." He tries to fill hearts with fear and despair so that if he can't get us to do things his way, and we're determined to follow God, at least we'll do it with long faces and turned-down mouths and hearts empty of joy.

One of my favorite poems is by Amy Carmichael, because it speaks of a concern I'm sure nearly everyone can relate to. It begins with the following lines:

> Far in the future
> Lieth a fear,
> Like a long, low mist of grey,
> Gathering to fall in dreary rain,
> Thus doth thy heart within thee complain;
> And even now thou art afraid, for round thy
>   dwelling
> The flying winds are ever telling
> Of the fear that lieth grey,
> Like a gloom of brooding mist upon the way.[9]

I would ask you: What is the fear that lies "like a gloom of brooding mist" upon *your* way? What disillusion? What disaster? What loss? What unhappiness? What misery is out there waiting for you? Does it soak up all your joy and empty your heart of all rejoicing? Do you have that fear?

I'm sure most people can immediately put a name to that fear "that lieth grey...upon the way." I'm sure those "flying winds" around your dwelling are filled with the whisperings of Satan, and they're "ever telling"—morning, noon, and especially in the middle of the night when you awake—of the fear that lies grey, the brooding mist upon the way.

God doesn't want us to live that way, doubting if He's there, doubting if He'll take care of us. God doesn't want us to be anxious, troubled, despondent, despairing. God wants us to rejoice. "Rejoice in the Lord always," Paul writes. "Again I will say, rejoice!" (Philippians 4:4).

Amy Carmichael concluded:

> But the Lord is always kind,
> Be not blind,
> Be not blind
> To the shining of His face,
> To the comforts of His grace.
> Hath He ever failed thee yet?
> Never, never: wherefore fret?
> O fret not thyself, nor let
> Thy heart be troubled,
> Neither let it be afraid.[10]

We must trust in Christ. As you walk down that way, you're protected by that trust, that faith in Christ. It seems that the gray "brooding mists" dissolve as you walk into them.

Recently some friends and I were discussing a problem that seemed to lie in our way. One of them said with something of a twinkle in his eye, "I knew a preacher who years ago said, 'Worry is interest we pay on a debt we may never owe.'" It's tough to preach to people who remember your sermons like that. (It's even worse if you have a wife who's related to elephants and never forgets anything you ever said from the pulpit.)

> Worry is interest we pay on a debt we may never owe.

Let me be the first to say I've never learned to apply perfectly all the things I've said from the pulpit. That's why it's always good to preach a sermon to the mirror before preaching it to the congregation.

Is there some trouble flying around your dwelling and whispering to you of fear and robbing you of hope? I urge you to put your trust in God, and He will still those winds and silence that voice.

J. C. Penney, founder of the chain of retail stores that bear his name, was a Christian, but like many believers he hadn't fully learned the lesson of walking by faith. Though his business survived the economic crash of 1929, he had some personal commitments that were causing him great trouble and stress. The stress was so severe that it caused the dormant virus of chicken pox, which he'd had as a child, to spring to life again in the form of the very painful disease of shingles.

He was so crushed and overwhelmed by the constant pain and agony of this disease that he had to be hospitalized. That night in the hospital he was sure he wouldn't survive, so he wrote farewell letters to his wife and son, saying he knew death was knocking at his door and there was nothing in front of him but darkness and despair.

He finally went to sleep. The next morning he awoke to singing. Perhaps he thought it was the sound of angels and he was in heaven. But no, it was coming from the hospital chapel a few doors from his room. He managed to get up, put on his bathrobe, and shuffle into the chapel, where he heard a group singing the hymn "God Will Take Care of You." As he listened to the words, he was transformed. He said it seemed like the very hands of God reached down and took hold of him and lifted him out of the dark, dank coldness and blackness of a dungeon and placed him in the warmth and brilliant sunlight of His love. He knew the power of God was there; he knew God was going to help him; he knew God would never let him down. And his life was transformed.

He said later, "I am seventy-one years old, and the most dramatic and glorious minutes of my life were those I spent in that chapel that morning."[11]

If you truly hear the words of this hymn and believe them, your life could be transformed as well:

> Be not dismayed whate'er betide,
> God will take care of you;
> Beneath His wings of love abide,
> God will take care of you.
>
> Through days of toil when heart doth fail,
> God will take care of you;
> When dangers fierce your path assail,
> God will take care of you.
>
> No matter what may be the test,
> God will take care of you;
> Lean, weary one, upon His breast,
> God will take care of you.

> God will take care of you,
> Through every day, over all the way;
> He will take care of you,
> God will take care of you.[12]

Next time God seems absent from your life, when you need Him the most, and all you sense is a shut door, go to Habakkuk 3 and read verses 17–18:

> Though the fig tree may not blossom [no future],
> Nor fruit be on the vines [no income];
> Though the labor of the olive may fail [no regular paycheck],
> And the fields yield no food [no food in the house];
> Though the flock may be cut off from the fold [no savings],
> And there be no herd in the stalls [nothing left]—
> Yet I will rejoice in the LORD,
> I will joy in the God of my salvation.

Be joyful!

The only reason that saying those words to someone in suffering is not a cruel joke is that God *is* there. He'll see us through. He *does* care. He is good, and He is sovereign. There's a fullness of His grace that we can obtain only by being faithful and obedient in times of darkness and pain. God's pleasure and His smile are upon the children who love Him when it's hard to do so.

We experience His presence at such times when we thank Him, even for the difficulties. The Bible says to give thanks in all circumstances (see 1 Thessalonians 5:18).

CONCLUSION

One of the most dramatic accounts in the Gospels occurs right after the Transfiguration. (You can read the account in Mark 9.) When Jesus and His three close disciples (Peter, James, and John) came down from the mount after He was revealed in all His glory before their eyes, they encountered the rest of the disciples in a doleful state. These other disciples had been unable to exorcise a demon from a young boy whose father was at his wit's end. The father had tried everything and hoped Jesus could cure the boy. He asked Jesus to do something about it—"if You can."

Jesus responded in a way that rebuked the man's unbelief implied in that last phrase. Then the man responded, "Lord, I believe; help my unbelief!" (Mark 9:24).

If you know the Lord personally and have accepted Him as your Savior but sometimes feel doubt in your heart, remember that man's earnest cry: Lord, I do believe. Help me overcome my doubt.

14

The Prince
of Darkness Grim

He [the devil] was a murderer from the beginning,
not holding to the truth, for there is no truth in him.
When he lies, he speaks his native language,
for he is a liar and the father of lies.

JOHN 8:44, NIV

One of the reasons God seems hidden to many today is that the Enemy of our souls *wants* us to think that way. Let's consider an analogy from history. One way the Nazis were able to rule Germany and the territories they conquered was through propaganda. Joseph Goebbels was the notorious chief of Nazi propaganda.

Day and night the propaganda machine led by Goebbels pumped forth the lies. The Nazis controlled the media so thoroughly that it was a crime to listen to shortwave radio stations such as the BBC broadcast from London. Those who were caught listening could be punished and even executed.

I recently heard about one daring German lady who hid her shortwave radio in the oven. She would stoop over, stick her head in the oven, and quietly listen to the broadcasts from London, despite the risks. The BBC was committed at that time to giving an accurate picture, even if it meant reporting on setbacks for the Allies. Meanwhile, the news reports broadcast by the Nazis portrayed themselves as winning virtually the whole time.

Nazi propaganda against the Jews was nonstop. Imagine growing up in Nazi Germany and having no intellectual or spiritual framework with which to resist the propaganda against the Jews. Millions were brainwashed.

Satan is brainwashing millions with his messages today.

In the same way, Satan is literally brainwashing millions with his messages today: God is dead. God is hidden. Or if there is a God, He must be some kind of demon, in light of the state of the world today. Day and night, speech is poured forth that constantly impugns the character of God. Goebbels is a picture of the devil and his propaganda.

We all know God loves us—or do we? Some people harbor a twisted picture of God. They think He's out to spoil their fun. Others think God accepts them in their unrepentant state.

Recently a homosexual happened to view one of our television broadcasts that dared to mention that homosexuality is a sin (a sin from which sinners can be freed). He wrote a letter to me in which he said, "I am a Christian. My God is the same as your God. And you know what? He's fine with my homosexuality. He created me as an equal. No one can take that away from me."

Well, I hate to burst this man's bubble, but we cannot just make up Christian revelation the way we want it to be. We must recognize God as He has revealed Himself. In the case of this confused man, he's wrong that God made him a homosexual and approves of his homosexual lifestyle, just as He wouldn't approve of my lifestyle if I were cheating on my wife. (And it would be even worse if I were trying to justify it.) God's revelation in Scripture is not to be obscured by people's sin or the lies of the Evil One.

Thus, God is hidden in the minds of millions of people because they've fallen for the devil's propaganda. I love the way C. S. Lewis once put it:

> This universe is at war…. It is a civil war, a rebellion, and…we are living in a part of the universe occupied by the rebel.
>
> Enemy-occupied territory—that is what this world is. Christianity is the story of how the rightful king has landed, you might say landed in disguise, and is calling us all to take part in a great campaign of sabotage. When you go to church you are really listening-in to the secret wireless [radio] from our friends: that is why the enemy is so anxious to prevent us from going. He does it by playing on our conceit and laziness and intellectual snobbery.[1]

The devil and his minions are working overtime to obscure God's presence.

SATAN'S ORIGIN

Where did Satan come from? The Bible gives us some clues.

In Isaiah 14 and Ezekiel 28 we read about this one who was created as an angel of light whose name was Lucifer, the light-bearer, and how he became puffed up with pride, having been made the most powerful, the most brilliant, the most beautiful of God's angels. He decided he would be like God, so God cast him down, and Lucifer took with him a vast host of other angels who fell into a totally depraved condition of sin. Now they are known as demons.

How you are fallen from heaven, O Lucifer, son of the morning! How you are cut down to the ground, you who weakened the nations! For you have said in your heart: "I will ascend into heaven, I will exalt my throne above the stars of God; I will also sit on the mount of the congregation... I will ascend above the heights of the clouds, I will be like the Most High." (Isaiah 14:12–14)

God cast this proud one down. And now, filled with wrath, Satan seeks to destroy the powers of God, the kingdom of God, and all who love God.

Because of his hatred for God and for Christ, Satan exercises his vengeance against those whom God created. Thus, we're told to "put on the whole armor of God" (Ephesians 6:11). The Bible frequently warns us about this spiritual warfare, as in this verse: "In latter times some will depart from the faith, giving heed to deceiving spirits and doctrines of demons" (1 Timothy 4:1). Satan is a deceiving and seducing spirit. He seduces people into his grasp with wiles and subtlety and craftiness. His whole character is one of maliciousness and malevolence. His only desire is to destroy.

> Satan seeks to destroy the powers of God, the kingdom of God, and all who love God.

One of the greatest decisions anyone has to make is whether he's going to believe God and His promises or Satan and his promises.

Some believe that there are not only black magic and black witches but also good witches and good white magic. Anton LaVey, the high priest of Satanism, mocks this whole idea, saying there's no such thing as a good witch. He says those who proclaim themselves to be good witches are using the tools of Satan without giving him his due. "They are fools," he says.

Doctrines of Demons

It's interesting to note what the Bible says are some of the teachings of the seducing spirits and the doctrines of demons. What would you suppose them to be? Murdering children? Black Masses? Horrible orgies? Heinous crimes?

Listen to this description of demonic doctrines: "forbidding to marry, and commanding to abstain from foods" (1 Timothy 4:3). You see, these are very religious people, even ascetic in their habits, and yet God's Word says their views are the doctrines of demons. It makes no difference to a demon whether you're the high priest of the church of Satan or an ascetic, as long as you ignore the teachings of the Word of God.

Why do people follow demonic practices, especially such blatant activities as seeking out spiritual mediums? Because they find that their wishes and desires are granted by these mediums. No doubt a great deal of this is nothing but fraud, and many "mediums" are merely charlatans. Yet people who have scientifically investigated this subject have identified elements of this that are absolutely inexplicable by all known scientific laws. Things happen through the occult arts of witchcraft, black magic, and white magic that cannot be explained by the laws of nature.

A woman recently told me how she'd been greatly involved in witchcraft and black magic. She said she'd gotten into it by way of astrology, which she said is the way many are brought into the occult. It's like gateway drugs. You begin with something easy like marijuana, and then it's on to the harder stuff like cocaine and heroin. Many people begin with simple experiments in parapsychology, ESP, astrology, and tarot cards, and slowly, subtly, they're drawn into the occult.

One young couple told me about their experiences for a period of time in witchcraft and the world of the occult. They had lived in a commune of thirty people who practiced the occult arts. They brought me something, which reminded me of the story in the book of Acts where, at Ephesus, those who had practiced all sorts of magical and occult arts were converted to Jesus Christ and then brought their tools of magic and books of incantations before the apostles and burned them.

The couple presented me with a genuine, slightly used crystal ball. The young woman told me she had actually seen a person in the crystal ball. And the young man said he had seen the effects of a spell, of physical objects moving around the room and injuring another human being. When these people sought to conjure up a demon, they had conjured up a being that was visible to those in the room.

Thankfully, through the power of Jesus Christ, this young couple was freed from the power of the occult.

THEIR WISHES GRANTED—FOR A TIME

A woman who visited our church said that she had amazing power over other human beings when she was involved in the occult. She was exhilarated and excited about her power to influence other people and to see that her wishes and desires were granted. Soon, however, she found that she had no power over herself, and all sorts of terrible things began to happen to her and her family. In great fear she finally fled from the occult, wanting nothing more to do with it.

Those who have been involved in the occult find that Satan never gives anything for free. Any ability, knowledge, or power is gained by pain and blood. Nothing is free. All is for the purpose of death, destruction, and attempting to tear down God's kingdom. It's so dangerous. Therefore the Bible repeatedly forbids us to have anything to do with the occult. It's an abomination in the sight of God.

In the Old Testament theocracy, those who practiced such things were put to death. So also King Saul died, not only for disobeying the word of God, but also, as we read in 1 Chronicles 10:13, "because he consulted a medium for guidance" when he visited the witch of Endor.

Those who have been involved in the occult find that Satan never gives anything for free.

It's obvious that even "white magic" does not have God as its source, for God never does what He forbids. Therefore, the only other source for such things is found in Satan and his demons and fallen spirits. Those who become involved in these things are opening themselves up to powers they don't understand and with which they can't deal.

The irony is that people involved in the occult believe they're in control. An incantation often ends with "As I will, so it must be." Contrast that to the Christian prayer "Your will be done." Little do the practitioners of the occult realize that occultism advances Satan's will, not their own, and they are merely his tools in the process.

GATEWAYS TO THE OCCULT

A spiritualist may use all sorts of religious phrases. He may use the name of God, the Trinity, Jesus Christ, or the Holy Spirit. But since a spiritualist is engaged in doing something God repeatedly condemns and forbids, it's obvious he or she isn't doing it by the power of God. This shouldn't be surprising, since Scripture tells us that "Satan himself transforms himself into an angel of light. Therefore it is no great thing if his ministers also transform themselves into ministers of righteousness, whose end will be according to their works" (2 Corinthians 11:14–15).

In all forms of spiritism or spiritualism (*spiritism* is the name used when it's atheistic or natural in its tendencies; when it wraps itself in religious garb, it's known as *spiritualism*), the person, by becoming passive, opens himself up to an unseen world he knows little or nothing about, a world containing powers in which he's merely a pawn.

In the Old Testament, we read how a single angel destroyed tens of thousands of Assyrian soldiers in one night. Shall we dabble with such as these? I don't merely wish to excite your imagination or to indulge your curiosity; I want to warn you of a very real danger and of the subtlety of him who, by turning himself into an angel of light and by his wiles and craftiness, slowly draws people into the occult—the kingdom of darkness.

After the popularity of the movie *The Exorcist,* in which a young girl became demon possessed through various occult activities beginning with the simple use of the Ouija board, the sale of Ouija boards skyrocketed despite the fact this motion picture portrayed all sorts of terrible things as a result of using it. Why? I think there were two reasons.

- The natural, unsaved man has a hunger for the supernatural and the unknown and desires to find it. Since he hasn't found it through Christ and is ignorant of the gospel, he seeks it in the occult world.
- Many people really don't believe it at all. For them it's just a game. They're playing at games, but they're like children playing with fire; they don't know what forces they're opening their hearts and minds to in the occult.

Some who saw *The Exorcist* said they realized for the first time the tremendous powers that exist in the real world of the occult and its demons. The Ouija board, like astrology, is one of those supposedly innocent things that can serve as a gateway to the occult.

The Bible teaches that Satan is real. He's a spiritual being, completely malevolent, the father of lies, and a murderer from the beginning. He seeks to defeat God by bringing about our destruction. "Well," you might say, "I'm not a Satanist. I have no intention of visiting Anton LaVey's church. I'm not interested in witches. I don't even consult my horoscope."

That doesn't matter. You may be every bit as much in the hand of Satan, though you have nothing to do with the occult. Christ came into a world that the gospel says lies entirely in the hands of the Evil One. The Bible says that Satan, the god of this world, has blinded the minds of people, lest the glorious light of the gospel of Christ should smile into their hearts and minds and they be redeemed from the bondage of Satan.

You may be every bit as much in the hand of Satan, though you have nothing to do with the occult.

BONDAGE THROUGH FEAR OF DEATH

Scripture also tells us that Satan has kept the whole world in bondage through fear of death.

Do you want to know if you're in bondage to Satan? Then think about how you would answer these questions. Are you afraid of death? When lying upon your bed at night, and in those times when your thoughts leap ahead to that day when you shall breathe your last, does the thought of a future world fill you with awe and dread? Is it a matter of darkness and mystery?

Or can you say, "I *know* I've been redeemed; I *know* I've been transformed; I *know* I've become a new creature in Jesus Christ; I *know* I have eternal life and am on my way to heaven"? If you don't know these things, you're absolutely in bad shape.

But thanks be to God, there's a stronger One than he who holds the world in bondage—One who has entered into the strong man's house and has bound the strong man and now despoils him of his goods, sets the prisoners free, and liberates those enslaved by the habits of sin. Jesus Christ came into this world to destroy the works of Satan, and this He did. True, Scripture says Satan is a lion that goes about seeking whom he may devour. But there came a time outside the city wall of Jerusalem when the Son of God hung upon a cross, apparently a hapless victim. Then out of hell there came forth with a roar that lion from the pit, who fell upon Christ and with claw and fang sought to devour this One whom he hated intensely. To his utter amazement, he found that here was One greater than Samson, who tore a lion apart. And this One, by His death upon the cross, defeated Satan, conquering the prince of darkness and setting his prisoners free.

Now we can be assured that we've been translated into the kingdom of God's dear Son. And where Christ was buried, there's now an empty tomb from which He arose. Now we have the power of the Holy Spirit coming to transform and renew those who were dead in sins.

We Tremble Not for Him

In his classic hymn "A Mighty Fortress Is Our God," Martin Luther notes:

> For still our ancient foe doth seek to work us woe;
> His craft and power are great, and, armed with cruel hate,
> On earth is not his equal.

Did we in our own strength confide, our striving
    would be losing;
Were not the right Man on our side, the Man of
    God's own choosing:
Dost ask who that may be? Christ Jesus, it is He;
Lord Sabaoth, His Name, from age to age the same,
And He must win the battle....

The Prince of Darkness grim, we tremble not for
    him;
His rage we can endure, for lo, his doom is sure,
One little word shall fell him.[2]

Someday soon one little word from Jesus Christ shall fell the devil and bring him down. For now, we must be cognizant of the Enemy's efforts (which are often successful) to obscure God from people.

CONCLUSION

Many years ago there was a Catholic lady who began to dabble in producing astrological charts. She found that she was quite effective in producing them. Friends and acquaintances asked her to produce charts for them, and she got deeper and deeper into this branch of the occult. But she reached a plateau from which she could never seem to rise. No matter how hard she tried, she could go no further in her horoscope charting.

Finally she made an appointment with a master in the field. Out of the blue, totally unexpected to her, he remarked that she needed to decide what she was going to do about Jesus Christ in her life. He wanted her to abandon any faith in Christ, however weak, and deny His deity. For the first time she saw astrology in a new light (or in a new darkness), and she repented and became born again in the process.

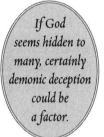

If God seems hidden to many, certainly demonic deception could be a factor.

If God seems hidden to many, certainly demonic deception could be a factor. The devil was a liar from the beginning. One of his big lies is that there's no God or that He's there but doesn't care or can't do anything.

Thankfully, in Christ we know God *is* there, and He does care.

Always remember: "He who is in you is greater than he who is in the world" (1 John 4:4).

15

If God Is Love,
Then Why...

I have heard of You by the hearing of the ear,
but now my eye sees You.
Therefore I abhor myself, and repent in dust and ashes.

JOB 42:5–6

I believe the most profound statement ever made in all of theology or philosophy is the simple statement comprised of three words—"God is love" (1 John 4:8). The height and depth and length and breadth encompassed in those small words are really beyond our comprehension.

Just imagine for a moment that God were *not* love. Suppose, instead, that God were a cosmic ogre, playing with people like grasshoppers in a bottle. Suppose God were a demon, filled with malevolent hatred, or suppose God were an impersonal force, like fate or some machine that had no feeling, no sympathy whatsoever toward mankind.

Those suggestions might make you stop to realize something of the significance of the words "God is love." Yet no person lives long in this world without that concept being challenged in his mind. This is especially true in times when we hear the screeching of brakes and the smashing of glass, followed by the smell of acrid odors in the intensive care ward. We sometimes wonder, *Is God really love?*

WHY ME, LORD?

This query has often been expressed in such questions as "Why me, Lord?" or the age-old observation that is the title of a best-selling book: *When Bad Things Happen to Good People.*

This book, written by Rabbi Harold Kushner, obviously touched something of a nerve, because it sold hundreds of thousands of copies. It takes us back to the book of Job, which sets forth three propositions that are assumed by most readers of Job: (1) God is all-powerful; (2) God is completely good, just, and kind; and (3) Job was a good man.

Most people have no trouble believing those things, either about Job's life or their own, especially when things are going well, as when Job was surrounded with his adoring family, and his flocks and herds were growing yearly. But then calamity struck again and again. Job's sheep, cattle, oxen, and camels were taken away, his servants were killed, his house burned, and his children destroyed. Finally, Job was stricken with boils and was left sitting on an ash heap. Suddenly all three of these propositions—that God is all-powerful, that God is all-good, and that Job was a good man—do not seem quite so clear.

A DILEMMA

How shall we solve this dilemma? Most of us at some point have come to a place where we easily identified with Job or felt that someone in our family was experiencing Job-like afflictions.

Why do bad things happen in the world? Rabbi Kushner reaches a certain conclusion on the matter. And while there are many things in his book that are touching—he writes frankly and candidly of a tragedy in his family, and he says some worthwhile things—I'm afraid I cannot agree with his ultimate conclusion.

Rabbi Kushner concludes that the author of the book of Job is ready to give up his belief that God is all-powerful. "God would like people to get what they deserve in life," Kushner says, "but He cannot always arrange it."[1] And this: "If God is a God of justice and not of power, then He can still be on our side when bad things happen to us. He can know that we are good and honest people who deserve better."[2]

Most of us have come to a place where we easily identified with Job.

In Kushner's opinion, the author of Job finds it difficult to flee to God for help and comfort, knowing that it's God who smites us. So he abandons proposition number one, that God is all-powerful.

This is somewhat reminiscent of the conclusion to this ancient enigma set forth by H. G. Wells, who reasoned that God obviously couldn't be both good and powerful and allow such evil to exist in the world. Wells said life was a great drama set forth on this world's stage, and all was going well until the hero of the drama stepped on the hem of the heroine's dress. She then stumbled over a table, which knocked over a chair, which struck a lamp, which fell and shattered and set the scenery afire. Suddenly everything was in chaos and turmoil, and people were running around screaming and shrieking. God, the stage manager behind the scene, was running back and forth doing His best to try to straighten things out. But, alas and alack, poor God: He just couldn't manage it.

Kushner goes on to say that Job isn't really willing to admit he's sinful in order to save God's reputation, so Job stands by his integrity.

KUSHNER'S ANSWERS NOT ACCEPTABLE

These conclusions may be some sort of a solution to the problem, but they hardly satisfy. We're left with a God who isn't really God, since omnipotence is one of the basic qualities and characteristics of deity. If God can't really control things, if He really isn't involved in the things of this life, what good, really, is He at all? Kushner's answer is that God does *not* control the events of this world but helps us to respond to them in a more positive way. What a letdown.

Not only is this conclusion not satisfying, it also plays fast and loose, I believe, with what the Scriptures teach. Notice what Kushner said: that he's willing to abandon the concept that God is all-powerful, and second, that Job isn't willing to admit he's sinful. Now compare those two statements with the actual facts in the Bible. The first thing Job said after God made His final appearance to him was "I know that You can do everything, and that no purpose of Yours can be withheld from You" (Job 42:2). Does that sound like the abandonment of an all-powerful God?

Clearly Job wasn't sinlessly perfect.

Job was supposedly unwilling to admit his own culpability or sin. But notice what Job says after God speaks to him at length out of a whirlwind:

> I have heard of You by the hearing of the ear,
> But now my eye sees You.
> Therefore I abhor myself,
> And repent in dust and ashes. (42:5–6)

Does that sound like Job was unwilling to admit his sinfulness?

But doesn't the Bible say Job was a "blameless" man? Yes, precisely, it does (1:1), but keep in mind that in Scripture this ascription of blameless perfection frequently conveys a meaning of "mature, godly." Job was unquestionably a godly and mature man, and he was far better than most of his contemporaries. But it's quite clear he wasn't sinlessly perfect. Nor does Job claim such perfection after God speaks to him.

What God Said

Throughout the book, Job says words to this effect: "O that I could come before the Lord, that I could question Him, that I could challenge Him, that I could ask Him to show me why I'm going through these things. What have I done that's wrong? Where have I lifted up my hand deceitfully? Where has my heart rejoiced over the adversities of my enemies? Where have I failed to give benevolence to the poor? Where have I fallen short? O that I could come before God and question Him."

At the end of the book, when God spoke to Job from a whirlwind in two long passages, what did God tell him? Did He say, "Job, this is what you did wrong" and "You were wrong here" and "Remember that beggar you didn't help over there?" No, God didn't say anything like that. He didn't say anything whatsoever about the questions Job raised. What did He say? He said, "Where were you when I laid the foundations of the earth?" (38:4). God described for Job a great stream of the things He had done and does daily—how He held constellations in His hand and how He created and controlled the greatest beasts—all to show Job how He is the great and mighty and glorious God.

Job responded, "I have heard of You by the hearing of the ear, but *now my eye sees You*" (42:5).

All God did was to reveal Himself to Job. When Job saw something of the infinite, brilliant, blinding purity and holiness and perfection of God, in all His glory, majesty, wisdom, and power, he said, "Therefore I abhor myself, and repent in dust and ashes" (42:6).

Didn't God punish an innocent man?

That's all God has to do. When we compare ourselves with ourselves, we go away deceived. But all we have to do is take one look at God, and we see how vile we really are. We look at perfection, we look at blinding purity and holiness, and we see the evil that fills all the crevices of our souls.

So much for Kushner's proposition three—that Job was good.

What about proposition number two—that God is completely good and just and kind?

There's a modern representation of the book of Job, a famous play by Archibald MacLeish entitled *J.B.* It's the story of Job in a modern business suit. J. B. has problems similar to those of Job, but he reaches a different conclusion. He decides God is *not* love, that God actually makes moral blunders and does things that are wrong. These shortcomings come through in the questions the play logically points to: Who is the hero—God or Job? Wasn't Job innocent? Didn't God punish an innocent man? Didn't God, therefore, do wrong? And therefore isn't God to be forgiven?

In discussing such issues at the conclusion of his book, Kushner says this: "Are you capable of forgiving and loving God even when you have found out that He is not perfect?" Kushner adds, "Can you learn to love and forgive Him despite His limitations, as Job does?"

Not What Job Did

But that isn't what Job did at all. What Job came to see was that God had no limitations and no imperfections whatsoever.

In my opinion it's completely blasphemous to say that God is someone we need to forgive. It's just as idolatrous to create such a deformed God in our minds as it is to fashion one out of wood or stone and worship it.

In answering the Lord, Job confessed that he had earlier uttered what he "did not understand" (42:3). Job realized the folly of his complaining. We fail to see that sin has blinded our eyes or that our jaundiced view of God is simply the result of our own iniquity.

As we saw earlier, Job was blameless only in the sense of being more mature and better than any of his contemporaries. He was what people call a good man, yet the best of men is still sinful. Job had attempted to justify himself and thus condemn God, and in his folly he uttered many foolish things. Finally he came to see this.

So, back to the original question: why do bad things happen to "good" people? The Bible says, "There is none righteous, no, not one.... There is none who does good, no, not one" (Romans 3:10, 12). So if Job was truly a "good" man, evidently his story must be from another planet, since there's no such good person in this world.

When we look around us, we notice people who, morally and ethically, stand head and shoulders above others. They seem so much more deserving than others. But when we look upward instead of horizontally, we see things differently.

There's one prayer you never want to utter: "Lord, give me what I deserve." If we received what we truly deserved, we would be cast immediately into hell.

Balanced in Eternity

In the book of Job, God blesses Job in the end, giving him back his home, giving him more children, and doubling the amount of wealth he had before. You should remember that in the Old Testament the blessings of God were of a temporal nature. In the New Testament they're more spiritual, and we're called upon to take the long view to understand that the things of this life will not be balanced until eternity. In heaven God has reserved rewards for us beyond anything Job ever dreamed of, and we should never lose sight of that promise.

In the book of Job, there's an underlying conflict between God and Satan. What does this conflict show about God's love and omnipotence? Satan believed that Job loved and honored God only because God was good to him and blessed him. Satan maintained that if all those good gifts and blessings were taken away, Job would curse God. So God allowed Job to suffer in order to prove that Job's love for Him was real. We see the triumph emerging early in the book: "Though He slay me," Job says, "yet will I trust Him" (13:15). At the end of the book, Satan's thesis is disproved. Job emerges battered and bruised yet still holding on to his belief in God's goodness, sovereignty, and love.

The Lesson for Us

We should remember that even though all of us deserve punishment for our sins, not every bad thing that happens to us is due to a particular sin. Encountering a blind man, the apostles asked Jesus, "Who sinned, this man or his parents, that he was born blind?" (John 9:2). His reply was, "Neither...but that the works of God should be revealed in him" (verse 3). Though sin is present in all the world, there are times when God brings difficulty that is not because of some particular sin but because He's testing us, even as He tested Job, to see if we will be faithful, even in the midst of trials and suffering.

Peter tells us that we shouldn't be amazed when the fiery trials come upon us. We should expect our faith to be "tested by fire" that it might come out as pure gold (see 1 Peter 1:6–7). Therefore God puts us through trials.

If God gave all His children wealth with ease, wouldn't everyone try to enter the kingdom simply for material gain? Our love for Him must be pure.

Bad things happen to us because we live in a fallen, sinful world. We've never been promised a trouble-free existence—only that He'll be with us in those troubles and give us the strength to endure.

Many years ago I went through a trial worse than anything I'd ever known. In the midst of it, many cries went up from my heart: "How long, O God?" But behind those cries was the belief that God was the sovereign Lord, that He was the infinite, all-powerful One who held the reins of the world in His hand. Even beyond that, He was a loving and merciful God, and I knew there was a purpose and a reason for all that happened. Furthermore, I believed that ultimately He would work all things together for my good.

CONCLUSION

We need to hold on to that promise, even if we don't see how it's going to happen in this life. We must learn to have a long view.

About a century ago a missionary named Dr. Henry C. Morrison returned to New York after spending forty years preaching the gospel in Africa. On the same ship, President Teddy Roosevelt was returning from a big-game hunting trip in Africa. Roosevelt was met with great fanfare: people cheered and waved flags, bands played, and reporters were eager to talk to him. But Morrison and his wife walked away unnoticed.

Morrison struggled with the injustice of it. A man comes back from a hunting party, and everyone throws a party. Yet Morrison and his wife had given decades of their lives to serving God, and no one seemed to care. Then it was as if the Lord put His hand on Morrison's shoulder and said, *But, Henry, you're not home yet.*[3]

Shadows Obscuring Our Vision of God

Blessed are the pure in heart,
for they shall see God.
MATTHEW 5:8

I f God seems hidden to us, then maybe there are things we're doing or not doing that obscure Him. Let's explore that further in this final chapter.

THE AGE OF POLLUTION

Our age has been called many things. It has been denominated the nuclear age, the atomic age, the space age, and the age of anxiety. But there's another designation that is altogether fitting and proper for the age in which we live, more fitting than ever before.

We live in the age of pollution. Pollution is one of the hallmarks of modern life. Of course, we've made great advances to clean up our environment, and certainly there are extremists who overstate the problem and overstate human contributions to pollution. Nonetheless, we face pollution in the air—we all know what smog is, biting and stinging and reddening the eyes. We battle pollution as well in our water. And even the ground is polluted with chemical and nuclear wastes. We have food polluted with innumerable additives and chemicals.

I recall many years ago flying into one of the industrial cities of the North. From the air I saw a huge, orangish cloud enveloping the city. I almost felt like trying to hold my breath the whole time I was there to keep from breathing the smog.

Later I was telling one of the inhabitants about how his city looked as I flew in. He said, "Oh no, that wasn't air pollution. That was caused by the orange lights we use to illuminate the streets."

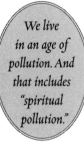

We live in an age of pollution. And that includes "spiritual pollution."

"But you don't understand," I answered. "I flew in at noon."

We live in an age of pollution. And that includes "spiritual pollution." A moral miasma has settled upon civilization today. It emanates from our books and magazines, the Internet, our motion pictures, our television programs, and our radio talk shows. It's found in the speech of individuals. It seeps up from so many places like noxious fumes corrupting and polluting the moral air we breathe.

While doing graduate study in New York in the 1970s, I recall a time when smog enveloped the city—a smog so dense that even from only a couple of blocks away, I couldn't see the Empire State Building. If it's true that a physical smog can block out something as vast as the Empire State Building, it's even more true that a spiritual smog—a moral smog—can block our view of God. No wonder we live in an age of doubt, an age of unbelief, an age of skepticism, an age of atheistic humanism. The moral fog of our time has blinded the eyes of people so that they're unable to see God.

We cannot see God through all the things of this world. We need solitude. We need time to be quiet in our spirits if we are to have any hope of hearing from Him or seeing Him. We must go away to a quiet place.

THE PURE IN HEART

Consider the words of Jesus: "Blessed are the pure in heart, for they shall see God" (Matthew 5:8). It's not to those with advanced degrees or expansive learning that the vision of God is granted but rather to those with holy lives and pureness of heart. I suppose that every halfway decent individual, every right-thinking person, has long been convinced of the truth of that verse.

Do we not instinctively know this? Is it really not innate within the human race that the threshold to the shrine and to the Shekinah Glory ever was and ever must be purity of heart? If we would see God, we must be like Him.

"We know that when He is revealed, we shall be like Him, for we shall see Him as He is" (1 John 3:2)—that is the promise of a future glory which shall be ours in that Great Day. But that promise is equally true in the here and now: those who are like Him shall see Him as He is.

Take a man who's corrupt in his nature, someone who has given himself over to vile and lascivious passions, who's perverted in his moral concepts, who's living for vanity and the baubles of this world, who's eaten up with selfishness and worldliness. Then introduce him to someone of pure character—a person with a pure heart, pure motives, and a love for God. That ungodly individual will not be able to understand the righteous person. He'll distort and pervert everything the godly person does. He will, indeed, impose his own vile motives on the godly person's pure actions.

"To the pure all things are pure," Scripture says, "but to those who are defiled and unbelieving nothing is pure; but even their mind and conscience are defiled" (Titus 1:15). To the unclean, all things are unclean, and the unclean can never see the great, pure God. If we would know Him, we must be like Him. The pure in heart shall see God.

BLESSED—TRULY HAPPY

The word *blessed* in its deepest and most significant sense means "happy," not with the mere happiness of the froth of waves dashed by the wind, but with a happiness extending to the depths of the sea. It's a deep calm, an abiding joy, an everlasting happiness. It's the joy that is at the right hand of God.

"Blessed," said Jesus, "are the pure in heart." Satan ever manufactures his lies and deceives the world with them. One of the most common lies today is the antithesis of this verse. We've heard it thousands of times. Hardly a day goes by when a message doesn't come from the very pit itself reinforcing the lie that blessed are the impure in heart.

"Happy are the exceedingly impure in heart," the world says.

Though Christ says, "Happy are the pure in heart," the world's message flies completely in the face of that. "Happy are the *exceedingly* impure in heart," the world says. "Happy are those who have HBO, especially late at night. Happy are those who see the most sordid films. Happy are those who drink in pornography. Happy, happy, happy are those who impress sordid images on their minds." This is the great message of the world.

You see it everywhere. Dump your wife and find another, and you'll be happy. You cannot be put in jail for just looking. A little impurity will make you a little bit happier. People who fall for those lies don't realize they're forsaking the greatest happiness in all the world.

There's a great Dutch painting of a little girl dropping a cherished toy from her hand. At first you're perplexed as to why she would let go of something so dear to her heart. But then, over on the side of the painting, you see a pure white dove fluttering toward her open hand.

And so it is with God. He would offer the dove of peace and love and joy, but too many people have their hands clutched tightly around some of the deceitful baubles of this world. The greatest happiness humanity can ever know—the happiness of seeing God—is lost through impurity of heart.

THE BEATIFIC VISION

The happiness of seeing God has been called the brightest star in the constellation of the Beatitudes. We spoke earlier about the medieval notion of the Beatific Vision, by which the mystics of the Middle Ages rejoiced in the concept of seeing God. The most blessed of all visions was to catch sight of God. It was the great quest of theology. It was the great pursuit of piety. It was the great mission of philosophy. It was even the original task of science—that through examining the cosmos, mankind would be drawn to see more clearly the Creator.

To see God means not merely to see Him with the physical eyes, for no one can thus see God, though many have sought to do so. One of the disciples said to Jesus, "Lord, show us the Father, and it is sufficient for us" (John 14:8). This was true not only of the apostles, but even pagan princes have sought the same thing.

The Roman emperor Trajan once said to a rabbi, "You teach that your God is everywhere, and boast that he resides among the nations. I should like to see him."

To which this rabbi responded, "God's presence is indeed everywhere, but he cannot be seen: no mortal eye can behold his glory."

Nevertheless the emperor insisted on seeing him.

"Well, suppose we try to look first at one of his ambassadors."

The Beatific Vision is seeing Him with the eyes of the soul.

With that, he led Emperor Trajan outdoors. The midday sky was bright and dazzling. The Christian bade the emperor to look up into the shining sun. Trajan protested, "I cannot. The light dazzles me."

The believer answered, "Thou art unable to endure the light of one of his creatures, and canst thou expect to behold the resplendent glory of the Creator? Would not such a sight destroy you?"[1]

The Beatific Vision is not seeing Him with our physical eyes but seeing Him with the eyes of the soul—to experience His joy and His peace, His serenity. This is what people are really searching for in life. They're searching for peace of heart and mind, for deep, abiding joy that only God can give them. This is the Beatific Vision. This is the great quest of life in all its parts. This is what God says we may have, but we can have it only in His way.

WHO SETS THE CONDITIONS FOR GOD'S REVELATION?

I recall reading about a young man in his midtwenties who was a complete unbeliever, yet he was troubled with the thought that there might be a God. So one day he walked into the forest. As he made his way through the pine trees, his thoughts turned to questions that haunted his heart and mind: Where did I come from? Is there a God, or is there not? If so, am I accountable to Him, or am I not?

He came at last to a small sandy spot where he sat down and continued his meditation. Then he fixed his eye on a small pine tree not far away. He said out loud, "God, if You're there, smite that tree, and I'll believe in You." He waited and watched. Nothing happened. He didn't realize that God is the One who sets the conditions whereby we may see Him and know Him. It's not up to us to dictate terms to God.

Several years ago I encountered another young man—a snarling skeptic—who happened to be present when I visited a high school and college youth group. He was a caustic unbeliever if ever there was one. I'll never forget his remarks: "Why, this is nonsense. What's wrong with you people? There's no God, and I'll prove it to you." Then he said, "God, if You really exist, strike me dead on the spot." The group became very quiet. Nothing happened.

I chuckled and said that he reminded me of a six-year-old boy going up to the boxer Muhammad Ali, who was world heavyweight champion at the time, and saying, "You think you're big stuff, don't you? But you aren't so tough. I can take you any day. In fact, if you want to prove you're the world heavyweight champion, let's see you knock me down." Muhammad Ali looks at him with something between a sneer and a laugh and walks away. The little boy says, "You see, I proved that Muhammad Ali is not the world heavyweight champion." Of course, he proved nothing of the sort; he merely proved he was a fool. His challenge was utterly beneath the champion.

Likewise, that young skeptic's challenge was completely beneath God, a God who had at one time swept the entire human race (except for eight people) into oblivion with a flood. Yes, God will set the terms.

A Heart That Is Cleansed

The requirement for seeing God is that we be pure in heart. What does that mean?

The word *pure* means that which has been cleansed, that which has had impurities removed from it.

In *The Idylls of the King* there's a story about a land ravaged by wild beasts that had slipped down from the mountains and destroyed children and adults alike. Finally a crusade was announced, and brave men took sword and spear in hand and went forth to destroy the ferocious monsters. At last the final beast was killed. As the *Idyll* expressed it, the land was cleansed once more; at last it was pure.

This is an interesting meaning for the word *pure*—to be rid of wild beasts. However, if we stop to think about it, there's a bit of the beast in all of us. In fact, deep down in the caves and caverns of the human soul, all manner of wild and ferocious creatures lurk. There's the lion of lust, the fox of deceit, the serpent of lasciviousness, the bear of boorishness, and many others in a veritable zoo that dwells in the human heart. If the land is to be cleansed, if we're to be pure, these creatures must be slain.

Another illustration of the meaning of the word *pure* deals with water. If water has been freed from all impurities so it becomes clear and transparent, then that water has become pure. So it is with our hearts. They're to be clear and clean and pure, like that water.

The Bible tells us, "Keep your heart with all diligence, for out of it spring the issues of life" (Proverbs 4:23). Jesus said it's what's in our heart that makes us impure (see Mark 7:20–23). Impurities are like drops of acid falling into a crystal-clear chalice of water.

There's the acid of pride, as we lift up ourselves and fail to call upon God or to show Him our gratitude. This corroding acid of pride, indeed, makes cloudy the water of our hearts.

There's also the acid of critical thoughts and critical talk. Some people cannot meet and talk with anyone about anything without finding someone to tear down or destroy, not realizing that each of these is an acid that beclouds the clear water of their hearts and prevents a vision of God.

This corroding acid of pride makes cloudy the water of our hearts.

There's the acid of impatience. Recently I was reminded of that as I felt the drops dripping in my own soul. By nature I'm a very impatient man; I want to get it done, and I want to do it now. But I realized such an attitude of impatience is really a critical attitude toward other people; it's a condemning attitude toward those who don't go at the speed we'd like. Such an attitude of impatience really deprives our hearts of any serenity or peace and any vision of God.

There's the acid of anger—the most corrosive acid, indeed. We cannot see God at all when our hearts are angry.

There are also the acids of jealousy and envy. When we're envious or jealous of other people, how opaque becomes the water through which we would see God.

There's also the acid of negative and unbelieving thoughts—doubts that obscure our vision of God.

All these prevent us from seeing God. They prevent us from having the joy, peace, love, and serenity God wants us to have.

I would make a plea for purity of heart—to you, to myself, to all of us. In a world beclouded with a moral miasma, there's a tremendous need for purity.

How beautiful is a single white flower blooming in the midst of a black, dank swamp. How beautiful is a life given over to holiness and purity, a life that's determined not to be part of the corrupted and polluted world around us. It's a life that will see God.

CONCLUSION

Can a human being know God? Yes, we've already seen that. The Lord says He's to be found when we seek Him with all our hearts. We can know Him, and we can be connected to Him. But even though the darkness of this world may obscure Him, His light can reach us, and we can live in it, here and now.

However, one day we shall see Him in all His glory—not only in nature, not only in His Word, but face to face. Then our faith will be reality, our hope will be fulfilled, and His love for us will shine upon us, and we shall know Him fully as we are known.

Who's in Charge?

Remember the former things of old, for I am God,
and there is no other; I am God, and there is none like Me,
declaring the end from the beginning, and from ancient times
things that are not yet done, saying, "My counsel shall stand,
and I will do all My pleasure."…
Indeed, I have spoken it; I will also bring it to pass.
I have purposed it; I will also do it.

ISAIAH 46:9–11

I s God truly hidden?

He may seem that way to some, but if you know Him, He's not hidden at all. Jesus Christ has made Him known. Jesus reveals the Father. Jesus Himself is God.

Furthermore, Jesus is at work behind the scenes. He is sovereign over history. The noted theologian Helmut Thielicke, in his book *The Waiting Father,* says this:

When the drama of history is over, Jesus Christ will stand alone upon the stage. All the great figures of history…will realize they have been bit actors in a drama produced by Another.[1]

Christ is the sovereign Lord God and has all power and all authority given unto Him by the Father. And what a glorious thing that is.

Many have attempted to challenge the supreme sovereignty of God, and indeed some have thought *they* were sovereign. King Louis XIV of France said, "I am the state." Kaiser Wilhelm of Germany was slightly more humble, saying, "Me and God." (That's bad grammar and worse theology.)

I recall an atheist who for some reason was mad at Christ. He said that if he met Christ, he would want to beat Him with a stick. (That's a scene I would like to witness. Wouldn't you?)

Here's what I would suggest to him. First, he ought to find the biggest stick he can pick up, then fly about ninety-three million miles up to the sun in the heavens and beat that sun into smithereens. That would be a pretty fair warmup for taking a stick to Christ.

Think about who Christ is:

- He's the second person of the eternal, almighty, triune God.
- He's the omnipotent One who has all power.
- He is One who does His will among the armies of heaven and inhabitants of the earth.
- He is One who stretches forth His hand, and there is none who can stay it or say to Him, "What are You doing?" (Job 9:12).
- He is One for whom nothing is too hard.
- He is One who created this universe and could create another universe tomorrow and tomorrow and all the tomorrows of eternity and would never run out of strength.
- He is One who is the infinite, omnipotent, uncreated Creator of the universe.

Christ is the sovereign Lord of all. But some people do not like that idea. They don't like the thought that someone is greater than they are and that someone is in charge over them. They want to be boss. They want to be God—at least the god of their own lives. Therefore they refuse to accept that God really is God.

Surprising, indeed, when we stop to think of how clear the evidence is of God's sovereign coordination of every part of our lives—yet people don't see it.

Do *you* see it? Let me ask you a few questions:

- Did you ask to be born into this world? Were you consulted on the matter?
- Was it your choice that you be a human being and not a mollusk, for example? Perhaps you could have been a worm. Was it your doing that you're not? Was it your decision that you not be a bear when you were born? Or a spider? (Imagine your first thought being "How do I get these eight legs coordinated?")
- Was it your decision that determined your race? your sex? the place of your birth?
- Did you decide whether you would be a healthy child or whether as a tiny, crying infant you would be dropped somewhere and hear nothing but your own cries resonating off the metallic walls of your short-lived home in a garbage can? Was that your choice?

You had nothing to do with any of them. All those decisions were sovereignly made by the sovereign God of this universe. So you see, whether we like it or not, we face the divine, sovereign foreordination of all things every day of our lives, if we have the eyes to see and if we aren't too proud to acknowledge that there is a sovereign God.

Sovereignty is not an attribute of Christ or of God; rather it's a prerogative that arises out of God's attributes—in particular, the attribute of omnipotence. He is the One for whom there is nothing too hard, the One who can do all things, the One who does whatever pleases Him, the One who has no end to His power and His strength. He's the infinite, omnipotent One who holds all strength and power in His hands—all of it—infinite amounts of it.

SOMETHING GOD CANNOT DO

There are wags who try to think up things that God cannot do. Well, there *is* something God cannot do: He cannot do evil. He cannot act contrary to His own nature. Therefore He cannot lie, He cannot deceive, and He cannot be immoral or unjust or unrighteous. He can do none of those things because He is holy and righteous and just and loving and kind and merciful and gracious.

Thank God He always does what is right.

Whatever He does, He does according to who He is. He has the power to do anything He wants to do. And thank God He always does what is right.

Think for a moment about this: suppose the devil—a being of vast malice and evil and wickedness and hatred—was God. Suppose a being such as that held in his hand all the power in the universe. If that were the case, we would be afraid to get out from under our beds, lest he see us and decide to exercise his malice against us.

That's something to think about, isn't it? But thank God that the devil is not God and that our sovereign Lord is loving and gracious and kind and all-powerful and good.

A Trip to Hell

Think again about the argument commonly heard: "No, it's not possible for God to be both all-good and all-powerful. Otherwise we wouldn't have the pain and sin and misery and chaos we have in this world." Actually, the opposite is true. To demonstrate that fact, let me take you on a little trip—to hell.

Look around, for there in hell you find such chaos, misery, and sin, such anguish and pain and crying out, as you've never begun to see in this world.

As you view those who are undergoing such damnation, may I point out to you that if God were not all good, He wouldn't care what sins these beings had committed in their time back on earth. That would be of no interest to Him. In fact, if He were evil, He might have rejoiced in their sin and given them great places in heaven rather than sending them to hell.

On the other hand, if He were not all-powerful, then surely all these evildoers condemned to hell would have united and would have overthrown God's power so they could escape from that dreadful place.

You see, it's precisely because God is both all-good and all-powerful that suffering and pain and chaos exist in any world where there are sinners.

It's against the background of evil that we can best see goodness.

We don't need to fear this One who has unlimited power, who is not only all-powerful but also omnipresent. He is everywhere present. We cannot escape from Him. There's no way we can hide from Him. He sees us in the night as clearly as in the day, wherever we go. If we ascend into heaven, He is there, the Bible says; if we sink into the depths of hell, He's also there (see Psalm 139:8). We cannot hide from Him; He is everywhere.

And He never changes. We cannot in any way alter Him. He is forever infinitely just and infinitely holy. And He forever hates sin. Let me make it more specific: He hates *your* sin with an infinite hatred, as He hates mine. He hates *all* sin. But thank God He loves us with an infinite love.

Because He is the sovereign Lord, Moses could go before Pharaoh eighteen times and challenge him to let God's people go. Throughout the Scriptures, every kind of tremendous victory was won because people believed in an omnipotent God who is greater than any earthly tyrant. We can rejoice in Him.

Handel's *Messiah,* that glorious, wonderful oratorio, climaxes with the famous "Hallelujah" chorus. As you've heard that refrain— "Hallelujah! Hallelujah! Hallelujah! Hallelujah! Hallelujah!"—have you ever wondered, *Why? Why the hallelujahs?*

Why the hallelujahs?

Because "the Lord God Omnipotent reigns!" (Revelation 19:6). That's why. So we can join with the heavenly multitude, whose voice is "as the sound of many waters and as the sound of mighty thunderings" and proclaim, "Alleluia! For the Lord God Omnipotent reigns! Let us be glad and rejoice and give Him glory" (19:6–7).

Does the thought of the unlimited sovereignty of God frighten you? Does it worry you? Does it fill your heart with trepidation that He can stretch out His hand and do whatsoever He pleases, and there's absolutely no one who can stay Him?

We should tremble before Him. It's right to fear God. The powerlessness we feel in a severe thunderstorm is only a shadow of His might. Not to fear God is foolishness, for it is, after all, "a fearful thing to fall into the hands of the living God" (Hebrews 10:31).

Then what a wondrous thing it is that this awesome God so clearly loves us. Indeed, "God is love" (1 John 4:8). And in clearly revealing Himself through His Son, Jesus Christ, God the Father also unmistakably discloses His love: "In this *the love of God was manifested toward us, that God has sent His only begotten Son* into the world, that we might live through Him" (1 John 4:9).

Therefore, when people reject Christ, as they're wont to do, is it God's fault that they then go on to a depraved and darkened mind and complain that God is hidden to them?

Not at all.

May God be true and every man a liar.

Soli Deo gloria.

Notes

Introduction

1. Kenneth Poppe, *Reclaiming Science from Darwinism* (Eugene, OR: Harvest House, 2006), 284.

2. Blaise Pascal, quoted in James M. Houston, ed., *The Mind on Fire: An Anthology of the Writings of Blaise Pascal* (Portland, OR: Multnomah, 1989), 150.

3. Words by Reginald Heber, 1826.

4. Pascal, quoted in Houston, *The Mind on Fire,* 117.

5. C. S. Lewis, *Letters to Malcolm Chiefly on Prayer: Reflections on the Intimate Dialogue Between Man and God* (San Diego: Harcourt, 1992), 44.

6. George MacDonald, quoted in Frank S. Mead, ed., *The Encyclopedia of Religious Quotations* (Old Tappan, NJ: Revell, 1965), 381.

Chapter 1: Evidence for God

1. Mortimer J. Adler, ed., *The Great Ideas: A Syntopicon of the Great Books of the Western World,* 2nd ed. (Chicago: Encyclopedia Britannica, 1990), 1:433.

2. Eric Marshall and Stuart Hample, comps., *Children's Letters to God* (New York: Pocket Books, 1966).

3. Marshall and Hample, comps., *Children's Letters to God.*

4. Marshall and Hample, comps., *Children's Letters to God.*

5. James Reid, *God, the Atom, and the Universe* (Grand Rapids: Zondervan, 1968), 1.

6. Elizabeth Mehren, "Humans a Mere Afterthought, Evolutionist Says," *Cleveland Plain Dealer,* December 17, 1989.

7. Guillermo Gonzalez and Jay Richards, *The Privileged Planet: How Our Place in the Cosmos Is Designed for Discovery* (Washington, DC: Regnery, 2004).

8. Pierre-Simon de La Place, *Evidences of Revelation*, 7, quoted in D. James Kennedy, *Why I Believe* (Waco, TX: Word, 1980), 40.

9. de La Place, quoted in Kennedy, *Why I Believe*, 40.

10. John G. Jackson, *Man, God, and Civilization* (New York: Citadel Press, 1983), 151.

11. Joseph S. Exell, ed., *The Biblical Illustrator*, W. M. Taylor, *Commentary on Genesis 1* (Grand Rapids: Baker, 1975), 7–8.

Chapter 2: More Evidence for God

1. Augustine, *The Confessions*, trans. R. S. Pine-Coffin, Great Books ed. (Chicago: University of Chicago, 1990), 1.

2. Robert Jastrow, *God and the Astronomers* (New York: W. W. Norton, 1978), jacket flap.

3. Jastrow, *God and the Astronomers*.

4. Jastrow, *God and the Astronomers*.

5. Jastrow, *God and the Astronomers*.

6. Henry Margenau and Roy Abraham Varghese, eds., *Cosmos, Bios, Theos: Scientists Reflect on Science, God, and the Origins of the Universe, Life, and Homo Sapiens* (La Salle, IL: Open Court, 1992).

7. Norman L. Geisler and Frank Turek, *I Don't Have Enough Faith to Be an Atheist* (Wheaton, IL: Crossway, 2004).

8. Ken Stephenson, "Does Evolution Disprove the Bible?" OU Christian Faculty and Staff, http://ourworld.compuserve.com/homepages/ouchristianfas/evobibl.htm.

9. Ravi Zacharias, interview by Jerry Newcombe, July 2007, Coral Ridge Ministries-TV, Fort Lauderdale. FL.

10. Robert T. Michael and others, *Sex in America: A Definitive Study* (Boston: Little, Brown, 1994), 127.

11. Paul Johnson, *Intellectuals* (New York: Harper & Row, 1988), 214.

Chapter 3: Atheism: Religion of Fools

1. Fyodor Dostoevsky, *The Brothers Karamazov*, trans., Andrew H. MacAndrew (Toronto: Bantam Books, 1970), 760.

2. Paul Johnson, *The Quest for God: A Personal Pilgrimage* (New York: HarperCollins, 1996), 14.

3. Will Durant, ed., *On the Meaning of Life* (New York: R. Long & R. R. Smith, 1932), PhilosophicalSociety.com, www.philosophicalsociety.com/Archives/Thoughts%20On%20Life.htm.

4. Richard Dawkins, *The God Delusion* (Boston: Houghton Mifflin, 2006), 176.

5. John P. Koster Jr., *The Atheist Syndrome* (Brentwood, TN: Wolgemuth & Hyatt, 1989), quoted in Patrick Buchanan, "Clay-Footed Gods of Atheism," *Washington Times,* April 24, 1989.

6. Friedrich Nietzsche, *The Antichrist,* quoted in Buchanan, "Clay-Footed Gods of Atheism."

7. Johnson, *The Quest for God,* 6.

8. Richard Morin, "Do Americans Believe in God?" *Washington Post,* April 24, 2000, www.washingtonpost.com/wp-srv/politics/polls/wat/archive/wat042400.htm.

Chapter 4: Is God Truly Hidden?

1. C. S. Lewis, *Mere Christianity* (New York: Macmillan, 1960), 51.

Chapter 5: Jesus: The Great "I AM"

1. Roy Hession and Revel Hession, *We Would See Jesus* (Fort Washington, PA: Christian Literature Crusade, 1958), 26.

Chapter 6: God Revealed in Christ

1. C. S. Lewis, *Mere Christianity* (New York: Macmillan, 1960), 154.
2. Personal note in D. James Kennedy's files: "Recent tribute from modern Jew, Solomon Freehof," for his sermon "Jesus Christ Our Lord," January 29, 1984.
3. Words by Edward Perronet, 1779.
4. Felician A. Foy, ed., *1988 Catholic Almanac* (Huntington, IN: Our Sunday Visitor, 1987), 199–200.

Chapter 7: How I Know Jesus Is God

1. "How America Sees Jesus" (Princeton, NJ: Gallup Poll, 1981).
2. C. S. Lewis, *Mere Christianity* (New York: Macmillan, 1960), 55–56.
3. Edward Henry Bickersteth, *The Trinity: Scripture Testimony to the One Eternal Godhead of the Father, and of the Son, and of the Holy Spirit* (Grand Rapids: Kregel, 1973), 28.
4. Alexander Whyte, quoted in J. Oswald Sanders, *The Incomparable Christ: A Doctrinal and Devotional Study* (Chicago: Moody, 1971), 68.
5. Napoleon Bonaparte, quoted in Frank S. Mead, ed., *The Encyclopedia of Religious Quotations* (Old Tappan, NJ: Revell, 1965), 56.
6. Earle Albert Rowell, *Prophecy Speaks: Dissolving Doubts* (Takoma Park, Washington, DC: Review and Herald Publishing, 1933), 123–26.

Chapter 8: Light from an Empty Tomb

1. Words by William Cowper, 1774.

2. Edwin Yamauchi, quoted in D. James Kennedy with Jerry New-combe, *Who Is This Jesus: Is He Risen?* (Fort Lauderdale, FL: Coral Ridge Ministries, 2002), 86.

3. D. A. Carson, quoted in Kennedy with Newcombe, *Who Is This Jesus,* 93.

4. Josh McDowell, quoted in Kennedy with Newcombe, *Who Is This Jesus,* 93.

5. Paul L. Maier, quoted in Kennedy with Newcombe, *Who Is This Jesus,* 93, 96.

6. N. T. Wright, quoted in Kennedy with Newcombe, *Who Is This Jesus,* 95, 96.

Chapter 9: How to Know God

1. If you would like more information to help you get grounded in the Christian faith, write to Coral Ridge Ministries, Box 40, Fort Lauderdale, FL 33308, and ask for *Beginning Again.* Coauthor Jerry Newcombe highly recommends a book that has helped him. It's a three-year, through-the-Bible study guide entitled *Search the Scriptures,* edited by Alan Stibbs (Downers Grove, IL: InterVarsity, 1974). It's now out in paperback.

Chapter 12: Luther's Quest for God   •

1. "Theologians Debate Luther's Beliefs," *South Florida News/Sun-Sentinel,* November 26, 1983, 4D.

2. "Lutherans and Catholics Reach Some Surprising Agreements," *Christianity Today,* December 16, 1983, 44.

3. Will Durant, *The Reformation: A History of European Civilization from Wyclif to Calvin: 1300–1564,* vol. 6, *The Story of Civilization* (New York: Simon & Schuster, 1957), 369.

4. Philip Schaff, *Modern Christianity: The German Reformation,* vol. 7, *History of the Christian Church* (Grand Rapids: Eerdmans, 1980), 59.

5. Schaff, *Modern Christianity,* 304–5.

6. "Lutherans and Catholics Reach Some Surprising Agreements," *Christianity Today,* 44.

Chapter 13: Doubts About God

1. Erwin Lutzer, *Ten Lies About God* (Nashville: W Publishing, 2000), 88.

2. Charles Hodge, *An Exposition of the First Epistle to the Corinthians* (New York: Hodder & Stoughton, 1857), 193.

3. Paul C. Vitz, *Faith of the Fatherless: The Psychology of Atheism* (Dallas: Spence Publishing, 1999), dust jacket.

4. Vitz, *Faith of the Fatherless,* 28.

5. Vitz, *Faith of the Fatherless,* 32.

6. Vitz, *Faith of the Fatherless,* 21.

7. Vitz, *Faith of the Fatherless,* 22.

8. William J. Murray, *My Life Without God* (Eugene, OR: Harvest House, 1992), 4.

9. Amy Carmichael, *Toward Jerusalem* (Fort Washington, PA: Christian Literature Crusade, 1961), 8.

10. Carmichael, *Toward Jerusalem.*

11. S. I. McMillen, MD, *None of These Diseases* (Westwood, NJ: Revell, 1963), 98.

12. Words by Civilla D. Martin, 1904.

Chapter 14: The Prince of Darkness Grim

1. C. S. Lewis, *Mere Christianity* (New York: Macmillan, 1960), 51.
2. Words by Martin Luther, 1529; translated by Frederick H. Hedge, 1853.

Chapter 15: If God Is Love, Then Why...

1. Harold S. Kushner, *When Bad Things Happen to Good People* (New York: Avon Books, 1983), 43.
2. Kushner, *When Bad Things Happen,* 44.
3. "The Missionary's Return," ad Dei Gloriam Ministries, addeigloriam.org/articles/stories/Morrison.htm.

Chapter 16: Shadows Obscuring Our Vision of God

1. Henry Mandeville, *Fourth Reader: For Common Schools and Academies,* Google Book Search, http://books.google.com/books?id=bHkSAAAAIAAJ&pg=PA79&lpg=PA79&dq=trajan+dazzles&source=web&ots=-9IdfhRosT&sig=8agZH_aFTx5zZW5uzUo2qxn3Xoo#PPA79,M1.

Conclusion: Who's in Charge?

1. Paul Little, *Paul Little's Why and What Book* (Wheaton, IL: Victor Press, 1980), 124.

Index

A NEW VIEW *of* THE OLD RUGGED CROSS

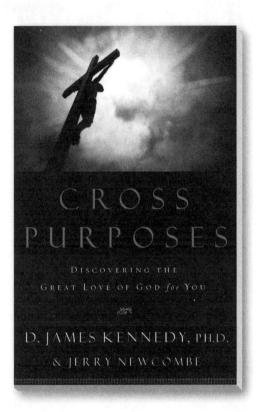

Let *Cross Purposes* spark a fresh revival of love in your heart for the One who cherished you enough to make the ultimate sacrifice. Each of the 48 short devotional readings will help you approach the crucifixion of Jesus Christ from a different perspective. Together they'll take you on a moving journey to the very core of your faith...to explore the truths that matter most in your life.

HOW YOUR FAITH SHOULD INFORM YOUR VOTE.

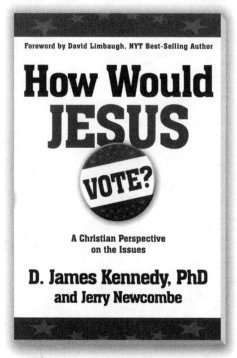

How Would Jesus Vote is a nonpartisan exploration of what God's Word says about the critical political issues of our time. You can apply your faith and biblical worldview to the ballot box and take a stand on the issues that will determine our nation's future.

 WATERBROOK PRESS
www.waterbrookpress.com